GINA PERKES

MASTERING THE ART OF
LONGARM QUILTING

40 Original Designs ❧ Step-by-Step Instructions
Takes You from Novice to Expert

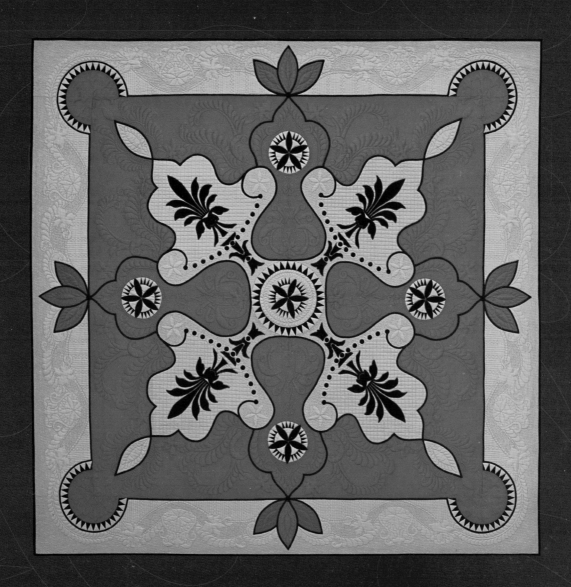

C&T PUBLISHING

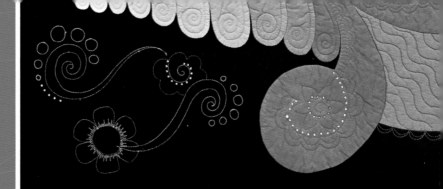

Photography and Artwork copyright © 2012 by C&T Publishing, Inc.

Publisher: Amy Marson

Creative Director: Gailen Runge

Acquisitions Editor: Susanne Woods

Editor: Deb Rowden

Technical Editor: Carolyn Aune

Cover Designer: April Mostek

Book Designer: Kerry Graham

Production Coordinator: Jenny Davis

Production Editor: S. Michele Fry

Illustrator: Aliza Shalit

Photography by Christina Carty-Francis and Diane Pedersen
of C&T Publishing, Inc., unless otherwise noted

Published by C&T Publishing, Inc., P.O. Box 1456, Lafayette, CA 94549

Library of Congress Cataloging-in-Publication Data

Perkes, Gina, 1974-

  Mastering the art of longarm quilting : 40 original designs, step-by-step
instructions, takes you from novice to expert / Gina Perkes.

    p. cm.

  ISBN 978-1-60705-410-8

1. Machine quilting. 2. Quilting--Patterns. I. Title.

TT835.P35218 2012

746.46--dc23

                                    2011029376

Printed in China

10 9 8 7 6 5 4 3 2 1

ACKNOWLEDGMENTS

Thank you to C&T Publishing for inviting me into your
family of authors. To my editor, Deb Rowden, thank
you for your patience and guidance. This has been an
incredible journey and learning experience.

Thank you to Gammill for your continued support and
encouragement and for producing a quality machine
that allows me to happily create without frustration.
You are a company filled with integrity and innovation,
and I am honored to represent you.

Thank you to the extraordinary longarm artists—
innovators of this ever-changing industry—who have
given me encouragement, friendship, and inspiration:
Linda V. Taylor, Linda McCuean, and Sharon Schamber.

DEDICATION

This book is dedicated to my family. I was truly blessed with the most incredible family a person could hope for.

To my husband, Chris: Thank you for providing me with a life that allows me to pursue this crazy passion of mine that I am often overcome by. Thank you for understanding that I have an innate need to create and an unstoppable desire to be good at it.

To my children, Rylie, Dalton, and Dillon: You are my gifts from above! Each one of you has been blessed with a creative heart that I hope to nurture with each new day. You inspire me daily with your creative outlooks and intelligent views of our awesome world. Thank you for keeping me company while I work—driving trucks with their wheels wrapped in thread, building Lincoln Log homes, listening to music, reading books—always next to me while I frantically attempt to meet impossible deadlines.

To my mother, Debbie: You have the most beautiful, optimistic spirit. You have always led me to believe that I could accomplish absolutely anything. Anything!

To my grandmother Arleen: Thank you for introducing me to the wonderful world of sewing and for your unfailing patience, encouragement, love, and friendship. I treasure our relationship.

CONTENTS

INTRODUCTION

Creativity has always played a very important role in my life. As far back as I can remember, I have always loved doodling, painting, crafting … creating. Though I am not formally trained in art, I consider myself an artist. Longarm quilting became my preferred medium when I discovered it at the International Quilt Festival in Houston in 2000. The machines just sat there on display, eagerly waiting to meet their new owners, happily willing to be auditioned. As I tested the machines, I realized that longarm quilting was just like drawing or doodling. The fabric was a blank canvas, the possibilities endless.

I began quilting for others to supplement our income while staying home to raise our three children. My youngest child was just six months old when I began longarm quilting. I would work while he napped. I quilted as a business for six years and finished nearly 2,000 quilts for my clients. Looking back, it was practice with a paycheck, training for the future.

I fell in love with creating quilts for show after four years of "practicing for pay." I soon realized that I simply didn't have the time to raise a family, quilt as a business, and create quilts for show. I decided it was time to stop quilting for others and to devote my spare time to quilting as an art form. I've been creating show quilts for nearly a decade now, feeding both my creative needs and my competitive drive. Creating quilts for show has driven me to improve the technical aspects of my work while stretching my creativity.

Once all my children were in school full-time, I decided to give teaching a try and soon found that I had another passion to add to my collection. I love spending time and exchanging ideas with others who share my quilting obsession, which has led to another exciting accomplishment—this book. I hope that you enjoy the ideas that follow and that they help you discover your inner artist.
Happy quilting!

Getting Inspired

Finding Your Inner Artist

Quilting is an art form—that is a reality increasingly recognized and accepted. As a quilter, you are an artist. Your canvas is fabric, your medium is thread, and your paintbrush is a needle. Many quilters underrate their work and creative abilities, claiming to be "not artistic." The truth is that the majority of quilters are drawn to the craft by their creative side (something they may or may not realize). Once we quilters accept that we are indeed artists, we can allow ourselves to grow creatively. For creative growth to happen, one must be inspired. All artists draw their inspiration from somewhere. In this chapter, you will discover how to get inspired by both the natural and man-made worlds. You will learn how your own unique style can begin to emerge in your work.

You are an artist. Accept it. Own it. Create!

Developing the Eye of a Child

We can learn so much from the children in our lives. It is often said that parents will learn more from their children than they will actually teach their little ones. I have found this to be true. As the mother of three children, I am amazed by them daily and strive to be like them in many ways. Have you ever noticed the awe in young children's eyes when they see something for the first time? They aren't hindered by the daily rush and overpacked days as adults are. They constantly observe the small details in their world: colors, shapes, textures, shadows. And just as quickly as they allow themselves to be fascinated by these details, their minds absorb this information like sponges.

As an artist, developing a childlike eye and mind will greatly benefit your work. I am a firm believer in multitasking and am guilty of overpacking my days and agenda. I am not suggesting that you spend an hour a day walking through the forest collecting leaves and acorns, though you may choose to do this occasionally for inspiration. But in the daily hustle and bustle of life, keep a childlike eye and mind as you perform your daily chores and duties. Both your natural and man-made worlds are swarming with beautiful shapes, textures, and colors, just waiting to make their way onto your next quilt!

Stop ignoring the beauty of your world in your daily routine! Develop a childlike eye, observing your surroundings with wonder and enthusiasm.

The Natural World

Nature is a great place to start when developing your eye and absorbing design possibilities. One of the best qualities: It is 100 percent copyright free. You can begin right in your own neighborhood. As a multitasker, I love the benefits of exploring my natural world in search of new quilting ideas. Here are just a few of those benefits:

Taking a short walk provides you with exercise and loosens up those muscles that tend to become strained from tedious quilting.

Sunlight and fresh air can improve your mood and outlook, which aids in the flow of creative juices.

Observing and appreciating your surroundings can release stress, which can inhibit creativity.

If it is not possible for you to take a walk or hike outside (for health or other reasons), simply sitting on your front porch and observing your world is greatly beneficial to your health and well-being. You can also get inspired as you drive or travel (though you should be sure to focus on the road and remain safe). My car is practically my second home as I constantly deliver kids to and from school, practice, and other places. If something catches my eye, I simply pull over to examine it further.

Be sure to vary the time of day in which you set out on an inspiration expedition. Observe the angle of the sun and the way it affects the appearance of most objects. If you are on a mission to find awesome textures for fill designs, landscape quilting, and so on, you will be the most successful when the sun is hitting your subject from the side. This is referred to as side lighting and showcases an object's texture beautifully.

On the other hand, if you are in search of the shape of a flower for a basic quilting design, begin your hunt when the sun is overhead and casts shadows directly on the ground. The shadow itself, free of details and texture, is where you will learn how to complete the shape in your quilting designs. Experiment with the effects of the sun by studying the same flower every three hours—you will be amazed at the significant changes in its appearance.

Textures become beautifully evident when an object is lit from the side.

Shadows provide a useful map of an object's outer shape, free of details and texture.

The Man-Made World

The work of creative people can be inspiring—sometimes overwhelmingly so. To copy a design is to simply reproduce the original artwork of another. To get inspired is to become enlivened or influenced by another's original artwork.

You have to be careful to familiarize yourself with copyrights so as not to infringe upon them. While some people find copying to be a form of flattery, others may take offense and/or even legal action. If you plan to closely reproduce the work of another artist in your own, contact her (or him) and ask for permission before you do so.

However, a plethora of inspiring shapes and textures in the man-made world may be free of copyright, such as those found in architecture, furniture, dishes, masonry, fabric design, fashion, home décor, and so much more. I have been known to become completely invigorated by the wallpaper in my dentist's office, the carpet pattern in a hotel lobby, or the tiles innocently resting atop my table at a favorite restaurant. It is as though the designs are screaming, "Help me to become a quilt!" As you practice developing your eye, you will start to see quilts everywhere, and you may need to wring out your mind sponge, which will be overflowing with amazing motifs and border and fill designs!

Ornaments, not just for Christmas anymore …
coming to a motif near you.

Jewelry, not just for adorning ourselves …
use it as inspiration for designs to adorn your next quilt.

Don't close your eyes until you have observed the details of your pillow or bedding fabric. After doing so, you might be visited by a creative quilt dream.

Exercises for Capturing Inspiration

Though your mind sponge is completely capable of absorbing an overabundance of ideas that spark your creativity, it is a good idea to begin organizing this fabulous material. You will want to have an inspiration cache close at hand to refer to frequently—especially when it's time to put those ideas to work.

Photographs

Taking photos of your fantastic finds is a quick and easy way to record them. There is no need to purchase fancy photography equipment because sharp, high-quality images are not necessary. You are creating a starting point and reference—crisp details are not pertinent. In fact, most cell phones are equipped with a camera that is perfectly adequate. I always try to keep mine nearby so that I can conveniently snap quick shots of wallpaper, carpet, or perhaps restaurant tiles. I simply ignore the bewildered looks of other hotel guests as I record the floor in the lobby from two feet up.

As you accumulate photographs, you should begin organizing them. The simplest way to organize your photos is with your computer. Create a new folder where your inspiration can wait until you are ready to use it. If you use a film camera, when you process your film request a disk of your images so you can upload them to your computer. If you don't get along well with computers, your printed photos can be placed in an album instead.

Take photographs of anything that evokes creativity. If the inspirational object is attached to a person, simply ask permission to photograph it. Most people are happy to oblige.

Sketches

I have a bit of a sketch pad obsession. Sometimes I purchase them, but my budget-buster side usually takes over, resulting in my perfectly suitable homemade versions. I usually buy copy paper by the ton and share it with my children. A plain white sheet of paper is an invitation for creativity that I enthusiastically accept.

These blank canvases must be kept close at hand. You never know when a commercial for area rugs will interrupt the nightly news, screaming, "I could be a block motif!" Just grab the sketch pad you keep on your end table and jot down your idea. Keep sketch pads in your purse, car, and nightstand drawer. Many artists are fortunate to be visited by designs in their dreams. If you are one of these lucky people, you will want to record your quilt dream immediately.

Sketch pads are a must-have for recording ideas that present themselves throughout day-to-day activities.

Inspiration Box

Often, inspiration comes in the form of a three-dimensional item: a fabric swatch, a plate, a tile, and on and on. You need a convenient place to store these items where you can revisit them often. Organization and storage accessories are easily available, which will make the task easier. You could use a small plastic storage container, a lunch box, a photo storage box, a tin, a shoe box, an empty paint can, or anything else you can find that has a lid and plenty of space.

Be very specific in your notes to yourself when you encounter an object that inspires you, or else when you revisit the object, you may find that you have forgotten its initial appeal. Or you could discover new details that interest you!

An "inspiration box" for storing three-dimensional items.

Bulletin Board

A bulletin board can be a very useful addition to your quilting space. Boards are available in a variety of sizes and styles, at reasonable prices. I change the contents of my bulletin board based on my current project. I refer back to my photos, sketch pads, and inspiration box, and then tack the items that relate to my current work onto the bulletin board. This practice lets me step back and view the design ideas from a broader perspective.

Install a bulletin board on a convenient wall for frequent glances. Fill it with all of the collected inspiration that is pertinent to your ongoing project(s).

Catalogs

Thumb through your favorite home décor or clothing catalog with a pen and a pad of sticky notes next to you. When you come to an item that captures your interest, examine it thoroughly, noting what specifically caught your attention. Was it the color, the shape, the texture, the dimension? Get more specific as you progress, making detailed notes to refer back to. Tear the page out of the catalog, stick your notes on it, and add the item to your inspiration box.

Subscribe to catalogs galore. Your mailbox will become an overstuffed supply of new ideas awaiting you!

Subscribe to catalogs galore. Stores will be happy to oblige your request to admire their products. They don't have to know that you don't plan to buy. Your mailbox will become an overstuffed supply of new ideas awaiting you!

Books of copyright-free designs are a great starting point for design creation and inspiration.

Inspiration in a Pinch

When you first begin the journey toward creating your own designs, you may encounter bumps in the road. There may be sections of your quilt that just don't seem to be speaking to you. If a deadline is nagging at you and you can't afford to set your work aside, it might be necessary to use available designs. Beautiful quilting designs that might suit your needs perfectly are easily obtainable and—when purchased—are completely legal to use in most applications. The predesigned quilting motifs of other artists can also be a great starting point for your own designs. Adding your own elements can make a design more appropriate for the given space as well as give it a touch of your own style. By combining your creativity with that of another, you begin to exercise your artistic side, which will lead to confidence in the design department.

Even with the mélange of quilting designs at your fingertips, you still might require something more. Copyright-free design books, such as those produced by Dover Publications, have come to my rescue at times like this. Such books affordably provide designs for any subject matter or in any style you could possibly imagine. The only problem I have found when referencing these inspiring books is brain overload. Some books contain more than 1,000 designs, all of them free of copyright.

Quilt Interpretation

Learning to interpret an unquilted top will help you achieve greater success in the visual and functional outcome of the piece. It is important to remember that all of the elements work together to form the finished product—a beautiful quilt!

I like to compare the quiltmaking process to making salsa: All of the ingredients mesh, complement each other, and result in a delightful gift to the palate. Instead of tomatoes, peppers, onions, and cilantro, your quilt ingredients include a top design, fabric, piecing or appliqué, and quilting. Some folks may enjoy spicy salsa so they throw in a few extra habaneros, just as some quilters, like me, are drawn to the machine-quilting aspect so they add a few thousand extra stitches! It all results in a sensory delight that is pleasing to the individual.

Making a quilt is ... a bit like making salsa!

Quilt Function

First and foremost, you need to determine the ultimate function of the quilt. If you quilt for others, ask your clients this question and make a note of their intent.

Utility

Utility quilts are created for use. Though I cringe when folks refer to my quilts as blankets, a blanket is exactly what a utility quilt mimics. It is meant to be snuggled with, slept under, dragged around by toddlers, picnicked upon, and of course, napped on by your best friend Rufus. Basically, a utility quilt is a hard worker that is paid well with love, travel, and play. As a result, a utility quilt will require a great deal of washing, and it needs to hold up to wear. When making one, you can ensure strength by minimizing stops and starts, and by selecting a thread that is built to last. Generally, a utility quilt has a shorter life expectancy than, say, a show quilt. So when you plan your quilting, don't underestimate the power of what one of my favorite customers used to call "quick and dirty" quilting.

If you allow your best friend to rest on it, that's a good indication the quilt is "utility" in function.

Wall or Decorative

Quilts epitomize comfort, warmth, and family, among other things. Simply by hanging on a wall, adorning the top of a table, or draping over the handrail to a staircase, a quilt can change the entire feel of the room it graces. Wall or decorative quilts are often created as seasonal décor, rotating in and out of use. Decorative quilts typically undergo less wear and tear than do utility quilts, although they might require occasional dusting or a visit to the washing machine after enduring a holiday meal, in the case of the tabletop quilt. These quilts are perfect candidates for showcase quilting, decorative threads, and plenty of stops and starts. Your techniques will be praised and admired by all who enter your home, the perfect reward for your hard work.

Show or Heirloom

Though not all quilters wish to travel the road showing their quilting, it is something every quilter should consider. The benefits of entering a quilt in a show are many. If nobody entered quilt shows, they wouldn't take place. Then where would thousands of people, including you and me, go every year for inspiration? Quilt competition is a positive motivator for improved workmanship, originality, and technique development. Though a win should never be expected, it is always possible, and what a wonderful perk to the process!

Show and heirloom quilts are attention seekers. They require a great deal of time to complete. The quilting should be dense, original, and well executed. A show quilt will not likely require a great deal of washing as it should be stored and handled with care. Accordingly, delicate threads and unlimited stops and starts can be used.

Quilts can make a great addition to your home's décor, fulfilling your "art needs."

Style

Fabric and color selection can have a great impact on the visual style of a quilt. Vibrant colors in a traditional setting can shift the style from traditional to modern. Similarly, an innovative top design can appear traditional in style if you use tamely colored calico prints. A middle-of-the-road quilt can be taken either way by the quilting designs. This is where your job gets exciting and your artistic side takes over. If it is a client's quilt, you can simply ask which direction the client would like to see the quilt head: artsy and wild or traditional and tame? If you are the owner of the top, you decide.

Traditional

Traditional quilts are popular and usually involve repeated pieced and/or appliquéd blocks. Additionally, traditional quilts may have open blocks alternating with pieced or appliquéd blocks, which offer a ready-made canvas for quilted motifs. Traditional quilting designs often include repeated motifs, such as feather, leaf, or flower shapes, accompanied by stippling or crosshatching.

Feathered Frenzy, 61″ × 61″

My quilt *Feathered Frenzy* is traditional in style. It includes repeated feathered block motifs surrounded by stippling.

Nontraditional

Many quilts fall into this category. Nontraditional quilts are often artistic or whimsical. These types of quilts are best enhanced with nontraditional quilting: unique textures, asymmetrical motifs, stylized feathers or flowers, and so on.

Untamed Splendor, 65″ × 65″

Untamed Splendor is an example of a nontraditional quilt.

To determine proper direction for my stitching paths along the faces in *Grape Harvest*, I referred to figure sketchbooks.

Landscape and pictorial quilts fall into the category of nontraditional quilts. One way to determine appropriate quilting designs and stitch direction for these quilts is to refer to instructional sketchbooks for artists. They are available at your local library. Using your needle, you can texturally enhance landscape and pictorial pieces in much the same way a sketch artist uses a pencil. If faces are involved, shapes can be enhanced by stitch direction, and shading can be mimicked by thread color or stitch density. For quilts depicting nature or architecture, go directly to the source with a camera or sketch pad in hand. When examining rocks, foliage, and wood, for example, remember to position yourself so that the object is lit from the side, as discussed in Getting Inspired (page 9). This way, the texture will become evident and a clear quilting pattern will present itself.

Comparing Design Styles

Compare the illustrations below. Each one represents quilting elements that can be incorporated into a block or border design or an allover pattern. Structurally, they are similar, but the shapes differ, changing the style altogether.

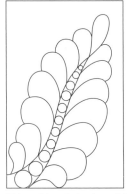

This quilting design is traditional in style. This simple double-stemmed feather design would be beautiful in a block or border design and would be fitting for a traditional quilt.

While the structure of this design is similar to that of the traditional example, it is nontraditional in style. With a simple change of the basic shapes used to create a quilting design, the overall style can be adapted to your project.

Fabric Choice

The fabric choices you or your clients make should play a major role in the planning of your quilting designs. Many beautiful fabrics can stand alone as art. However, if you plan to showcase your quilting skills, you will want to do so atop fabric that reads as a solid.

Solid-reading fabrics are a playground of potential. Visual balance can be achieved beautifully by incorporating solid-type fabrics with the delicious prints you have fallen in love with. Avoid stitching intricate designs over busy fabric prints, where your designs will only become hidden amid the fabric pattern.

Complex quilting designs require a significant time investment, so it simply doesn't make sense to spend loads of time and effort when your labors will be overshadowed by a busy fabric print. Invest your quilting time wisely. For a busy border, incorporate simple gridwork or loose meandering. These will lend texture to the fabric instead of competing for the starring role.

When quilting the solid-reading areas, let the designs of the print fabrics elsewhere in the quilt serve as your inspiration. Incorporating the design elements of one portion of the quilt into another will unify the piece and create visual interest.

Compare these fabrics:

Notice how the quilting designs become camouflaged by the busyness of this print.

This solid-reading fabric allows the quilting to play a significant role.

Block and Border Design

My Favorite Drafting Tools

- Mechanical pencils with plenty of lead refills
- Fine-point permanent markers
- Good erasers
- Paper—plain and tissue
- Copy machine (optional)

- Rulers—a variety of types, including a square quilter's ruler (to create the actual block size) and a flexible 18″ straight ruler (for sectioning). (See Rulers and Gridwork, page 64.)
- Lightbox (optional)
- Inspiration box (page 12)

- Scissors (for fabric and for paper)
- Thick transparent template plastic
- Erasable marking pen
- Transparent tablecloth vinyl (for larger designs)
- Solvy water-soluble stabilizer

Balance

As you begin the process of designing your own motifs and block-quilting designs, you need to be aware of balance. Quilting is successfully balanced when the stitch density remains consistent throughout the piece. I'm sure most of us have witnessed unbalanced quilts as we walk through local quilt shows. Generally, they don't hang well. They often appear wavy rather than flat. If you don't plan to incorporate filler quilting, then you will want your block and border designs to fill the spaces without leaving any large areas unquilted. However, if you plan to accentuate your motifs with fillers, you will want to leave some space to do so. This does not mean that your quilt needs to be heavily quilted or that all of your designs should be exactly the same size to obtain balance. Compare the balanced and unbalanced quilting designs at right.

Balanced quilting

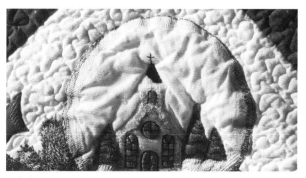

Unbalanced quilting

Photo Shoot

Unless I am quilting an allover design, I always take a photo of the quilt awaiting a visit to the longarm. If you have a design wall (page 90), simply pin the quilt up and shoot. Be sure to include the entire quilt. A straight-on angle will result in an image that is free of distortion. If you don't have a design wall, either tack the corners of the quilt to an open wall in your home using thumbtacks or lay the quilt on the floor and shoot the photo from above. You don't need a photography degree or a fancy camera for this; a simple point-and-shoot or even your cell phone's built-in camera will work.

Next, print several copies of the image onto plain copy paper, not photo paper. It is best to have the copies printed fairly large—8″ × 10″ should suffice. If you don't own a printer, you can have this done at your local one-hour photo developer.

The photos will serve as practice sheets for you to begin auditioning possibilities. The reduced image of the quilt enables you to create a design that enhances the entire quilt. When we view segments or folded-up portions of a quilt, the whole design looks indistinct. We tend to notice unsharp points or wavy borders rather than the overall shape and potential. By examining a full view of the quilt, the quilting path often presents itself. Secondary designs often become evident as well.

An 8″ × 10″ photo of your quilt can serve as a great starting point for auditioning designs. Print the photo onto paper so that you can begin sketching ideas directly on it.

Divide and Conquer

Simplification is the key to successful block and border design. When we become overwhelmed, our creativity and concentration can be hindered. Refer to the photo for the planned design structure. You are now ready to "divide and conquer" your spaces!

 TIP

Always begin your design drafting with a pencil. I prefer mechanical pencils because they offer a sharp point without the mess of sharpening. I keep a separate eraser at my side so I can quickly make changes to unsuccessful designs. When you have completed a design that will make the cut, trace over it using a permanent pen. I like to use fine-point black Sharpies, which provide a fine line and will not bleed at pauses.

CREATING A LIGHTBOX

A lightbox is a handy tool for both drafting designs and marking them onto a quilt top (see To Mark or Not to Mark, page 59). If you don't own a copy machine, a lightbox is also a must-have for the symmetrical block and border designing techniques described in this chapter. My homemade lightbox is a well-loved tool that I couldn't live without. Though it isn't graceful or high-tech, it gets the job done. If you aren't a do-it-yourselfer, feel free to purchase a lightbox. It is important that it is of sufficient size, at least 2′ × 3′, to allow adequate space for large border designs. Follow the instructions below to create your very own one-of-a-kind, bulky, yet lifesaving, lightbox. Feel free to customize it and spice it up; bedazzle it if you like.

1. Start by selecting a sheet of Plexiglas in your desired size, at least 2′ × 3′.

2. Cut 4 lengths of lumber (two-by-fours work well) based on the size of the Plexiglas. Allow for overlapping at the corners.

NOTE: Most large home improvement stores cut lumber at no charge. It is not necessary to miter the corners; simply overlap the pieces to save time.

MATERIALS NEEDED:
■ ¼″ Plexiglas
■ lumber
■ hardware
■ drill
■ screwdriver
■ 2 under-cabinet light fixtures

4. Lay the Plexiglas over the platform. Drill holes in the corners of the Plexiglas using a glass bit. Screw in place at each of the 4 corners.

3. Screw the lumber together at the corners to create a platform for the Plexiglas. Paint or decorate if desired.

5. Position the box over the 2 under-cabinet light fixtures. You're in business!

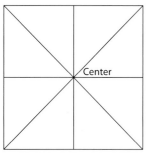

Divide the square into 8 equal segments.

Block Motifs

To create symmetrical block motifs that you plan to mark on your quilt later, start with a piece of blank copy paper.

Draw a square on the paper the same size as the intended block. Divide the square into 8 equal segments, diagonally, vertically, and horizontally. The point where the lines intersect is the center of the block and motif. Now you have 8 identical segments, only 1 of which needs a design.

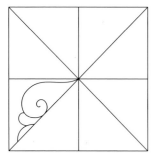

The design is on ⅛ of the block.

Create a design for 1 of the 8 segments. Remember to refer to your inspiration cache (pages 9–14) for a creativity boost.

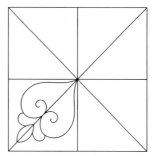

A mirror image completes the first quadrant.

Mirror-image your design using either a lightbox or a copy machine. Combine the original and mirror-imaged segments. This is the first quadrant of the block.

Repeat the quadrant.

Repeat the quadrant by photocopying or tracing, rotating as you go so that the corners and centers stay consistent, until the block motif is complete.

You will be amazed at the secondary surprises that will emerge from your original segment!

Spinning Motifs

You can set block designs in motion by making them appear to spin.

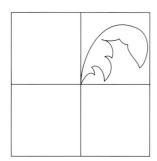

Divide the block into fourths, either diagonally or vertically and horizontally. Draw an arc that leans to one direction.

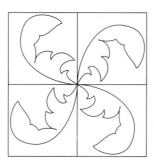

Rotate the original segment in the direction of the tilt, keeping the centers consistent. Trace the remaining 3 sections so you have a complete spinning block design.

 TIP

Spinning motifs are an excellent choice for pieced blocks in which the seams divide the block into sections.

Vases and Urns

Vases and urns can make a grand statement in your quilting. I have always admired the dimension and depth they add. They are especially appropriate for rectangular or large corner spaces. Quilting designs using vases or urns often graced the traditional wholecloth quilts created by our foremothers dating back to the 1700s. Their timeless appeal, not just in quilting but also in architecture, home décor, and other art forms, makes finding design inspiration an easy task. Collect images of vases, urns, or baskets you find in magazines, catalogs, or books.

Having several examples to refer to will help stimulate your creativity and provide a model for your drafting. Though they often appear elaborate, vases and urns are surprisingly simple to draft and design. I like to simplify urn design by separating the elements into three parts: the outer shape, the inner detail work, and the contents.

Outer Shape

Most often, I design my urns using side-to-side symmetry. The process is stress free and the results are stunning. However, urns don't have to be limited to symmetrical design. Some quilts, particularly artsy ones, simply don't welcome symmetry and repetition. But as a starting point for what will surely grow into a love affair, side-to-side symmetry is relatively simple. To create it, first determine how much of the block should be devoted to the urn and how much should be reserved for the contents. Half and half often works well. Treat the urn and its contents as separate designs to start.

Borrow pots from your house or garden to study their proportions and shapes.

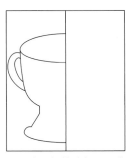

Mark off the portion of the block reserved for the urn and divide it in half vertically.

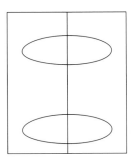

Draw 2 ovals—these will become the urn's base and top. Half of each oval will be disregarded, but I find accurate shapes are better achieved when initially drawn as a whole.

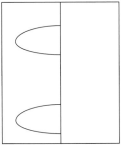

Choose your favorite side and then erase the opposite half.

Complete half of the urn shape, erasing the unnecessary upper portion of the base oval. Experiment with different outer shapes until you are pleased with the result.

Mirror-image your design. The outer urn shape is now complete and ready to be detailed and filled!

Inner Details

You will need to retain balance within your quilting designs. The outer portion of your urn will most likely be too expansive on its own, out of proportion with the rest of your quilting designs. As a result, you will need to add some details to the inner portion of the urn. You can use the same side-to-side symmetry technique as for the outer urn shape.

Create inner details for half of the urn. Make several copies of the outer urn shape so you can audition inner detail designs directly onto the urn.

Mirror-image your design. You are almost there; now it is time to fill this urn!

Urn Contents

Filling your custom urn is going to be more fun than you can possibly imagine! You are now ready to make this design a true centerpiece for your quilt. Take inspiration from the quilt itself for items to place into the urn. For example, if your quilt contains floral fabric, you may wish to mimic some of the flowers. If there is no evident theme, the sky is the limit. Flowers, leaves, fruit, birds, and feathers make great vase fillers. Try combinations and unexpected hidden objects for visual interest and personalization.

You may wish to use symmetry when filling your urn or toss symmetry out the window. Both options will produce equally gorgeous designs. If you have a large variety of objects to fill your urn, an asymmetrical design may be more appropriate. You are the designer, so have fun!

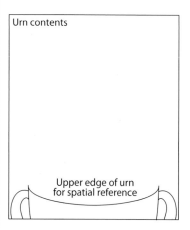

Urn contents

Upper edge of urn for spatial reference

Draw the remaining section of the block, the part reserved earlier for the urn contents. Leave several inches of space along the bottom edge of the paper so that you can trace the urn's upper edge for placement and design assistance. If a symmetrical design is desired, divide the sheet in half, top to bottom.

You may choose to have the urn's contents spill over the edge. This creates extra dimension. Fill up the urn with your heart's desire.

 TIP

Remember to study the elements that make up the quilt top for an idea boost or possible design theme. For example, if the quilt includes sections of beautiful fabric containing dramatic designs, trace the designs onto a transparency and include them in the contents of the urn.

Block Skeletons

I like to refer to this design technique as "skeletons" because it begins with a very basic shape that will later be enhanced and customized. This technique is perfect for lovers of free-hand quilting because minimal marking is required. Just one basic block skeleton can easily become a collection of very different block motifs.

Template Plastic

I keep about 10 sheets of thick, transparent template plastic in my stash of necessary supplies and tools. Template plastic is invaluable for use in many different applications. Because it is transparent, it can be positioned either directly over the actual fabric block or over a drawn paper block for sizing. Once you've sketched a design skeleton that you like on the plastic, cut it out using nonfabric scissors. The plastic shape can be traced repeatedly and then set aside for future use. I frequently refer to my collection of saved templates for new projects.

Place the transparent template plastic directly over either your presectioned quilt block or presectioned paper block. Draw a very basic shape on the plastic and cut it out.

Trace the template directly onto the quilt, using an erasable pen, or onto the paper block. Mirror-image the template to complete the quadrants.

Line this edge up with diagonal sectioning lines.

Block center

⅛ of the basic block skeleton design

If you'd like to begin your own collection, create a template using this basic block skeleton design. You can enlarge or reduce it to accommodate any block size. Mirror-image the template to complete a quadrant.

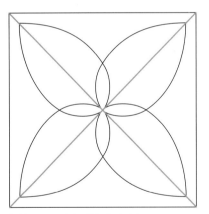

Basic, symmetrical block skeleton

Now you have a completed block skeleton that is waiting to be embellished with freehand details. Vary the details added based on the style of the quilt. You can further change the outcome of the motif by adding details to different portions of the skeleton (inner edge, outer edge, both edges). Compare the block designs on page 28. All began with the same basic skeleton. However, by varying the placement and style of the freehand details, I have created a collection of very different motifs.

This block design is perfect for a child's quilt with the addition of balloonlike hearts attached to wavy doubled strings. It can be stitched using a single start and stop. Begin at the center. First, stitch the 4 quadrant skeletons, ending in the center. To make the inner design, freehand a wavy line out toward the block corner, top it off with a heart shape, then stitch back down over the first wavy line, following it loosely, and end in the center. Repeat for the remaining 3 quadrants.

Fill the inner portion of the block skeleton with these alternating curlicue shapes. They can be backtracked loosely to create a design with a single stop and start.

Transform the block motif into a whimsical leaflike design with the addition of veinlike details in the inner portion of the skeleton and scallops along the outer edges.

Shape Combinations

For more variety, try combining multiple skeleton template shapes. They can be overlapped to create depth.

Combine different shapes for more variety.

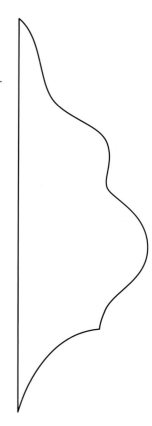

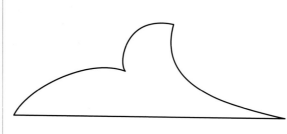

Use these templates to create block skeletons. Enlarge or reduce to fit, and add freehand details to suit your style.

You also can combine two shapes, varying their placement. To do this, place the first shape along the diagonal position marks and the second along the vertical/horizontal marks.

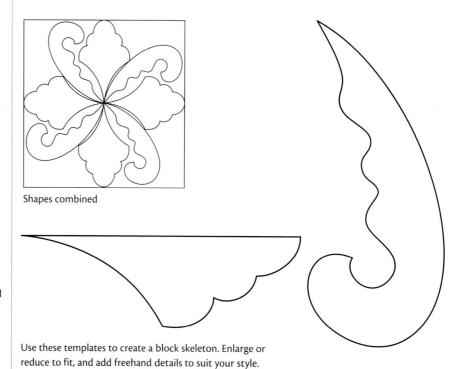

Shapes combined

Use these templates to create a block skeleton. Enlarge or reduce to fit, and add freehand details to suit your style.

Innovative Settings

Some quilts don't conform to the traditional alternate block settings. They may contain vast open spaces that rest alongside appliqué or curved piecing, making them more challenging to design. For these situations, I use transparent vinyl, which is usually used for tablecloths, to draft my patterns. The discovery of this product changed my world! So for a life-changing experience, run to your local fabric store, and pick up several yards of tablecloth vinyl. Then follow the steps below.

Use an erasable marker.

1. Position the vinyl over the quilt and mark placement indications, such as appliqué or pieced edges. Now you are ready to make the magic happen! It is important that you use an erasable marker for this step in case you get excited and your marks carry off the edge of the vinyl. You may wish to add masking tape to the edges as a precautionary measure that provides your eye with a stopping point.

2. When you are pleased with the designs you have created and feel that they enhance the quilt top, move the vinyl away from the quilt. Then trace over your marks with a permanent marker. This step provides a dark line that will show through the fabric nicely for quilt marking.

Move the vinyl away from the quilt, and then trace the marks with a permanent pen.

3. Place the marked vinyl on your lightbox. As an added bonus, the vinyl adheres to the Plexiglas on its own, so it is not necessary to further secure it with tape. You are now ready to mark the designs onto your quilt. For mirror-image applications, simply flip the vinyl over.

Appliqué Treatment

It is highly likely that you will encounter appliqué along your journey, especially if you quilt for others. Many quilters hesitate to quilt appliqué pieces because, most likely, a great deal of effort has gone into the appliqué design and construction. An allover quilting design is usually not a good choice for appliqué because it can detract from or compete with the shapes. Appliqué generally plays an important role in the overall appearance of the quilt and should be enhanced—not hidden—by the quilting.

When I approach a quilt containing appliqué, my first step is always to secure and enhance each appliqué element by outlining it using a fine monofilament thread. Sew-Art is my favorite thread for this task. It is virtually invisible, concealing the occasional stray stitch, which would be an eyesore if I were using colored thread.

When planning the next course of action, I always consider balance. Has uniform quilting density been achieved in the outlining alone? Most of the time, outlining will suffice. However, some appliqué shapes are open and free of inner detail shapes. While appliqué should lend dimension to the quilt, it shouldn't create imbalance. If unquilted portions are too large in comparison with the surrounding quilted designs, they will appear wrinkly.

So when quilting is called for, have fun with it! Try adding details relevant to the style and mood of the quilt. For example, enhance appliqué houses with quilted roof shingles, windows, or architectural texture. For a realistic effect, add vein details to leaf and petal shapes.

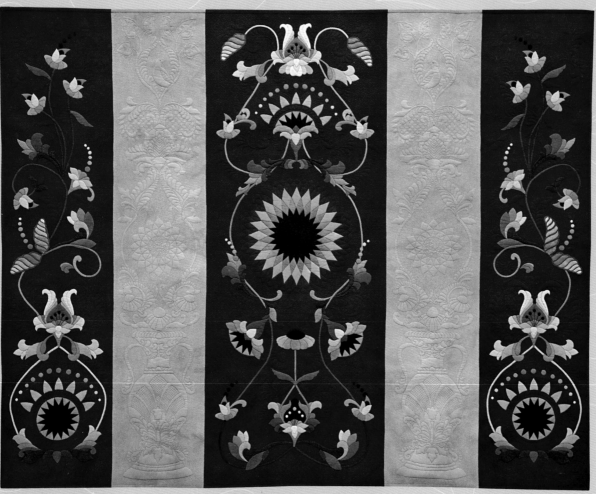

Tuscan Sun, 84" × 62"

Securing the appliqué elements of *Tuscan Sun* was sufficient to achieve balanced quilting and draw focus to the design.

Grape Harvest, 90″ × 50″

The large, expansive boxes used by the field workers to transport grapes in *Grape Harvest* required additional quilting to achieve a balance. I selected a subtle crosshatching design to add texture without taking over.

Borders

Borders can play a very important role in the success of a quilt. Sometimes they showcase a fabric that is simply too gorgeous to cut up for piecing. Other times they can create a blank canvas for us to show off our quilting skills. It is important to remember that fabric greatly affects what quilting designs you should or shouldn't choose. Before you plan an intricate border design, make sure your efforts will be rewarded.

 TIP

It is always best to be up-front with your clients concerning severely problematic borders. They may not be aware of their mistakes and would likely fix them if they were. Kindly offering instructions for proper border technique benefits both parties. When I quilted for others, I offered my clients an information sheet on border technique, backing preparation, and other important tips for preparing the piece for longarm quilting.

BUILD A BETTER BORDER

Generally, the addition of the borders is the last sewing step prior to the quilting. Oftentimes, quiltmakers become eager either to begin the quilting or to deliver the project to someone who will perform the quilting magic for them. As a result, they may hurry through this final step. The border application can affect many factors in the overall appearance of the quilt, such as how well it hangs, whether it is squared up, or whether it will pucker in the quilting process. To ensure that the borders will improve rather than harm the appearance of your quilt, follow these steps:

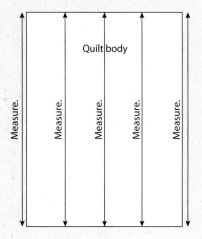

1. Measure the quilt from top to bottom at the center, the edges, and halfway between.

2. Determine which of these measurements is the smallest.

3. Cut the first 2 borders to this exact length.

4. Mark the quilt's side edges and the 2 border pieces at the centers. Then mark halfway between the center and outer edges.

5. Pin the border pieces to the quilt, right sides together, matching marks. Ease in fullness and stitch.

6. Repeat for the top and bottom, taking new measurements after the addition of the side borders. If you plan to include multiple borders, follow these steps with the addition of each new border.

If you quilt for customers who supply you with less-than-perfect borders, it may be necessary to ease in fullness along the borders as you quilt. Measure the quilt to determine whether it is squared up before planning your quilting designs. If the edges of the quilt are longer than the center, you may opt for a simple, loose design in the border. This will let you ease in the excess fabric as you quilt, avoiding puckers. In addition, a high-loft batting will help to fill out the extra fabric.

Symmetrical Borders

Square Quilts

As with blocks, borders can seem overwhelming when viewed as a whole. But when you section them off, similar to block drafting, the task is simplified to just a small portion to create. You will be astounded by the secondary designs that occur when your original design is mirror-imaged. Square quilts, those that are equal in height and width, lend themselves particularly well to this technique.

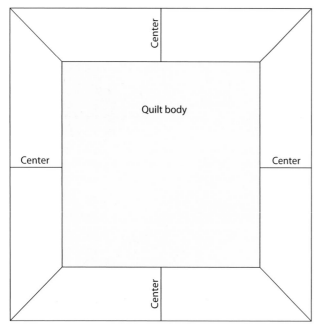

Divide the borders into sections.

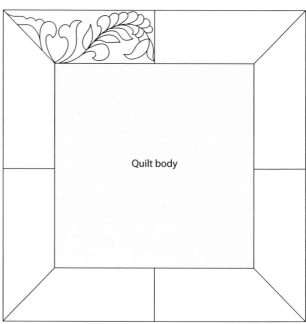

It is now only necessary to create a design for the small section. The borders will appear to radiate outward from the corners if you treat the corner like a block design and then branch off from it.

Mirror-image the design and then repeat it for the remaining sides. You now have a gorgeous, symmetrical border design.

 TIP

I draft my border designs using clear tablecloth vinyl (page 29). Its transparency and large size make it the perfect choice for easy border designs. I lay the vinyl over my border and mark the section I am designing, including inner and outer edges. Then I sketch my border design using a washable marker. When I am satisfied, I move the vinyl away from the quilt and trace over the finalized design using a fine-point Sharpie permanent marker.

Rectangular Quilts

Rectangular quilts, whose length varies from their width, are the most common. You can still simplify the design process by sectioning as discussed for square quilts. The result will be a symmetry similar to that of square quilts, but an additional design will need to be included to fill the extra space on the longer sides.

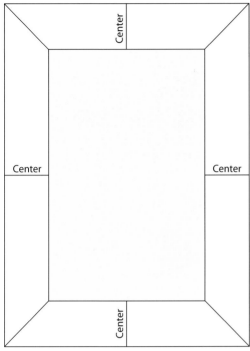

Divide the borders into sections.

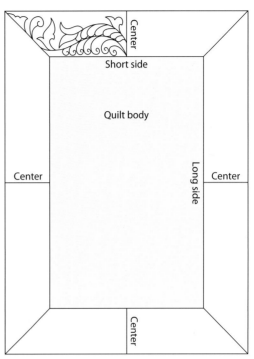

Draft a design for the border of the shorter sides. This particular design radiates outward from the border's centers.

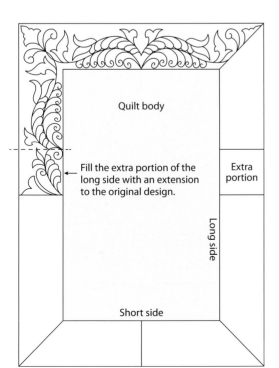

Mirror-image the original design and then extend it outward to fill the additional space of the longer sides. This new, extended design can be mirror-imaged and traced for a complete border design for the 2 long edges.

Completed semi-symmetrical border design

 # TIP

When you have a fairly clear idea as to the direction of the border design, audition possibilities directly on the fabric using a chalk pencil. Sometimes the first time's a charm. If you like the result and want to mirror-image and repeat it for a symmetrical result, trace your design onto transparent vinyl and then transfer it to the remaining border sections using a lightbox. The design can be easily mirror-imaged by simply flipping the vinyl.

Skeletons

If you are opposed to in-depth marking but seek a uniform design result, try this technique, which involves only minimal marking. Border design skeletons provide a shape foundation you can complete with the addition of various freehand shapes and styles. By substituting new freehand details, one border skeleton can be used to create many dramatically different border designs.

The skeleton shape can be designed on a separate sheet of paper or directly on the border. The foundation lines should flow gently along the border, shifting in direction periodically; some lines can branch off for added variety.

You may choose to travel the full distance of the border with the design skeleton or end it at the halfway point. If you opt to cut it short, trace the spine to the remaining half to complete the first border.

For a border design that travels in one direction, trace the skeleton to the borders so the second design follows the first, heading the same way. For a radiating effect, create a skeleton for the first half of the border, and then mirror-image it for the second half. Add connecting lines for rectangular quilts and for corners where needed.

With a map drawn out for you, you're ready to hit the open quilt road. Rev up your engine, put on some tunes, and enjoy the trip! Here are a few samples to fuel your creativity.

Border skeleton 1

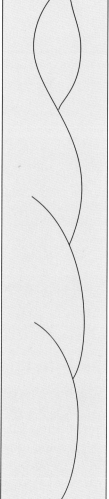

Border skeleton 1 with
added freehand feathers

Border skeleton 2

Border skeleton 2 with
added freehand whimsical
floral details

Border skeleton 3

Border skeleton 3
with added freehand
spiky details

Using Block Motifs in Borders

Block motifs can be used to create beautiful border designs. You can combine several block designs to fill the border and vary the direction of the motifs to create movement or other desired effects. Experiment by tracing the block motif repeatedly onto transparencies or vinyl squares and positioning them along the border. You can try a number of placement patterns—all of the designs pointed upward, turned away from the centers, pointed toward the centers, alternating up and down, or pointing in one direction around the quilt as shown in the example.

Sizing the Motif

1. When determining an appropriate size for repeated motifs, measure the width of the border, subtracting the seam allowance you plan to use for the binding. This measurement is the size that you should use to draft square motifs. For example, if the border is 6″ wide and you plan to use a ½″ seam allowance for the binding, you should draft the motifs 5½″ square. This way you can perfectly fit a motif in each corner.

2. Place or mark a motif in each corner and at the center of each side of the quilt.

3. Measure the empty space from the edge of a center motif to the edge of a corner motif. Divide this measurement by the motif size. For example, if you are using a 6″ motif and the open space measures 30″, you will need 5 motifs to fill the space. If the open space measurement is not evenly divisible by the motif size, you will need to either space the motifs out slightly or overlap them. If you separate the motifs, the empty space is usually minimal, but if you want the designs to connect, consider adding small connecting shapes, such as leaves, feathers, loops, or swirls.

Scalloped Borders

Scalloped border designs are very pretty and lend a lacy feel to a quilt. You can easily create your own custom scallop templates using the thick template plastic discussed in Part 1 of this chapter (page 27). I love to create my own templates. They are sized perfectly to my quilts' spaces and are inexpensive to create. Here is my basic scallop map-making technique that you are encouraged to further develop, alter, and make your own!

Determine the scallop style and approximate size(s) by placing template plastic or vinyl over the border and starting to sketch using a washable pen. Compare large scallops with small ones, pointy scallops with subtler ones. Alternate the sizes if you'd like. Play! Once you have determined an approximate size and style for the scallops, you can calculate the number of scallops needed and the exact size to cut the scallop templates. Follow the example described on page 39.

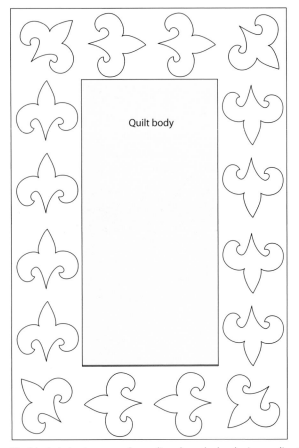

The block design is repeated, traveling along the border in one direction.

Evenly Spaced and Sized Scallops

For the example, I have selected a rectangular quilt and purposely chosen measurements that are not easily divisible. Many quilts are less-than-cooperative sizes in which we want to envision proportionate designs. The beauty of creating your own templates is that you can make them specifically suit a space of any size. This technique will help you feel comfortable creating evenly spaced designs for odd spaces.

1. Measure the seams that attach the quilt's borders to its body. These are the edges that the bases of the scallops will rest upon. My example quilt measures 49½″ × 69½″.

2. Based on your practice samples, estimate the number of scallops that will pleasingly fit along the border.

3. Divide the shorter seam measurement from Step 1 by this number. For example, if the seam measurement is 49½″ and you have estimated that you can fill the border with approximately 6 scallops, then divide 49½″ by 6. The result is 8¼″. So each scallop should be 8¼″ at the base for an evenly filled border design. If this measurement does not suit you (it is either too large or too small), simply divide the seam measurement by a new number. A larger number will yield smaller scallops and a smaller number will yield larger scallops.

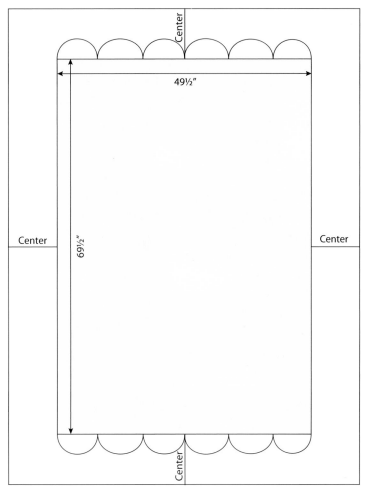

A little simple math indicates that to evenly fill the space of the shorter borders, 6 scallops, each measuring 8¼″ at the base, are needed.

If the quilt were square, we could stop here. For our rectangular quilt, however, it will be necessary to recalculate for the remaining two borders, which will be equal to each other in length but longer than the first two borders. The size of the scallops that can evenly fill the space of the last two borders may vary slightly from the size used for the first two. You can come very close, though, by using a little more math. Grab your calculator!

4. Divide the seam measurement for the remaining sides by the initial scallop measurement. My example has a long-edge seam measurement of 69½″, so I will divide 69½″ by 8¼″. The result is 8.42. This result indicates that I can fit approximately 8½ scallops at this measurement. Because I cannot use a half scallop, I need to do some more calculation.

5. To determine the size to make my scallops so they will provide an even fit, I have to estimate the number of scallops needed. If I estimate 8 scallops, I divide 69½″ by 8. I get 8.6875, or close to 8⅝″. These scallops will be ⅜″ bigger than the top and bottom scallops, but the difference will not be noticeable.

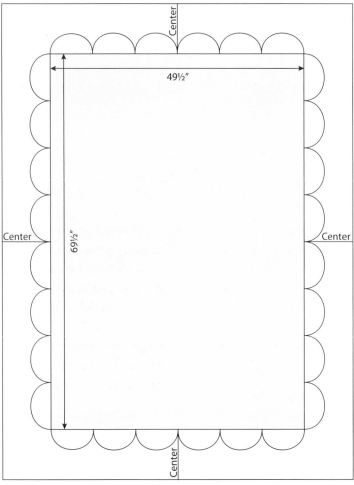

A bit more math determined that the longer edges of my quilt will require slightly larger scallop bases to fill the space evenly. This minor size variance is not noticeable to the eye.

Borders without Boundaries

Creating border designs that virtually fall off the edges of your quilt can be dramatic, adding unexpected flair. There are no rules stating that your designs have to be stitched out in their entirety. This technique is perfect for the freehand lover and nonconformist. For even more variety, extend the incomplete shapes inward toward the body of the quilt, cutting them off at the seams. The designs will appear to tuck themselves under the seams and then resurface unexpectedly. Large, obvious shapes—such as dramatic filigrees trailed by feathers or leaves—produce the best effect for this technique. Avoid placing the shapes in directional patterns. Random placement will add to the unconventional appeal of this technique.

There are no rules for this type of border design. If you want to mark the designs preload using a lightbox, begin with completed designs. Position them so that they extend beyond the quilt edges and inner seams, but mark only the parts of the design that fall within the borders.

Mark a border without boundaries preload.

Borders without boundaries can be easily included in your quilting postload by using Solvy water-soluble stabilizer (see Postload Marking, page 61). Trace the complete shapes onto the Solvy. Position the marked Solvy sheets on the border, allowing them to overlap the quilt body and fall off the edges unexpectedly. Secure the Solvy edges with pins. When quilting, remember to stop stitching when you reach the inner seams.

Quilt body

The border designs in this technique are unstoppable!

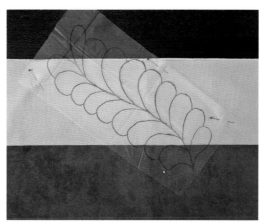

Mark a border without boundaries postload using the Solvy method.

Housewarming, 45" × 45"

The Freedom of Freehand

A longarm machine has the unique ability to be operated from both the front and the back. Many longarm quilters begin their journey at the back of the machine. Pantograph patterns, followed from the back of the machine using a laser stylus, are a great starting point for beginning longarm quilters. They offer an easy place to learn and become familiar with the general operation of the machine. Once you feel comfortable with the machine's basic operations and your own fluidity, though, it is time to advance. Don't be afraid to make that necessary progression to the front of the machine where your creativity can flourish!

Benefits of Working at the Front of the Machine

Design Placement

When you are facing the front of the machine, you are the boss! You are working with the quilt at your fingertips, whereas when you operate the machine from the back, the quilt is less visible and accessible. From the front, you make the executive decision of where and when a leaf, flower, or feather should be incorporated. You can simply meander along, placing appropriate designs in awaiting open spaces. Perhaps the quilt you are working on contains appliqué shapes in need of definition or details such as leaf veins, petal details, or texture. Originality and artistic customization take place at the front of the machine.

Heading Off Trouble

From the front of the machine, you can foresee possible problems and fix them before they escalate. For example, excess fabric en route to becoming a pucker can be eased in when working from the machine's front. Also, you're immediately aware of empty bobbins and thread breakages, a benefit that will save you from the frustration associated with quilting an entire row without thread.

Avoiding Monotony

In comparison with pantographs, which can be repetitive and monotonous, freehand work is spontaneous and fun. Creative diversity can be achieved with freehand work by varying designs throughout the piece. The more you shift from one shape to another, the more alert your mind will be.

Loosen Up!

Freehand work should be fun, almost therapeutic. Let your guard down, loosen up your muscles, and play, play, play! When you step from the back to the front of the machine, consider yourself to be stepping outside the box. Think of freehand quilting as a dance with your beloved machine. Lose yourself in the rhythm of its motor. When you practice, begin with large shapes; then as you master them, gradually begin shrinking them. Challenge yourself to see how small you can make a particular shape. Avoid gripping the machine's handles with a ferocity that creates white knuckles. Instead, grip the handles gently as you guide the machine along. The result will be smoother movements and happier muscles. Jerky movements are your enemy—unless, of course, you plan for zigzags! The beauty of freehand is that there are no rules.

Stitch Regulation

Many longarmers choose to invest in stitch-regulated machines right from the start. I was not one of them. I learned to quilt on a nonregulated machine and found that I was able to produce even stitches after a good deal of practice. I now own a machine with a stitch regulator but find I rarely use it. If you are accustomed to stitch regulation, I encourage you to visit the manual mode. You may find, as I have, that the hum of the machine in manual mode will help you find a rhythm that will result in design fluidity. In addition, I have noticed that some stitch-regulated machines provide even stitches only at certain speeds, particularly fast speeds. This makes stitch-regulated mode a great choice for allover patterns, which are generally stitched more quickly than customized work. Simply stated, stitch-regulated mode has its time and place, but you should be comfortable using manual mode as well.

Don't be afraid to try out your machine's manual mode!

Practice Makes Perfect

It has been wisely suggested that practice makes perfect. This is especially true with freehand quilting. Repetition brings about ease, and with ease comes success. Practice pieces don't need to be a financial hardship. You can purchase fabric or old sheets at your local thrift store inexpensively. For practice, it is not necessary to include all three layers of backing, batting, and top. Instead, just use one layer of scrap batting and a top piece. Community service quilts offer all the practice you could possibly hope for with a philanthropic benefit. Most local quilt guilds have stacks of pieced community service quilts awaiting a volunteer quilter.

Doodling on paper is another great way to practice freehand shapes and design possibilities.

With both drawing and quilting, the designs begin with your imagination and are created by your hand's movement. Practice is beneficial whether it is performed on paper or on fabric.

Try this exercise: Doodle on paper with a pen held in the palm of your hand the same way you would hold your machine's handles. Challenge yourself to create smooth designs with the pen held in this position. I always keep a small whiteboard and dry eraser marker at my longarm machine for last-minute warm-ups.

Hold your pen the same way you would hold your machine's handles.

Warm-Ups

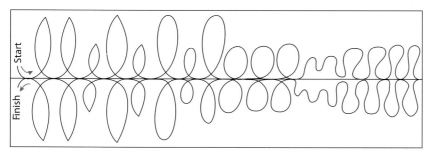

Freehand Basics

This exercise will acquaint you with the basics of freehand work. It is a great exercise because it combines pointed, rounded, and curved shapes as well as size variations of each. You may wish to mark two separate rows to stitch along. This will provide extra practice for following along edges in pieced blocks, sashing, borders, and the like. Avoid hesitating at pointed tips, as in the first leaflike design, especially when using manual mode. It is natural to pause before completing the second half of leaflike shapes, but this can result in uneven stitch buildup and often thread breakage. Once you have completed your first practice row, stitch back in the opposite direction, mirror-imaging the design.

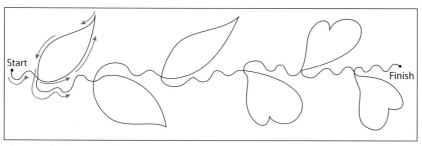

Alternate the direction of the shapes. Try incorporating other shapes as well as the two shown in the example.

Directional Shifting

With freehand quilting, it is important to become comfortable with directional shifts. For most applications, variations in both direction and size add visual interest and aid in avoiding inconsistencies. Here is a great exercise that will familiarize you with some basic freehand motions. For added benefit, stitch this same design horizontally, vertically, diagonally, and as mirror images of each. Once you feel that you have mastered the directional shift technique, try reducing the size for an added challenge.

Freehand work should be fun, almost therapeutic. Let your guard down, loosen up your muscles, and play, play, play!

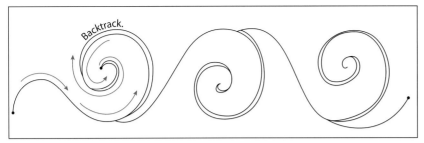

Create repeated curlicue shapes, backtracking outward from the point of the curl. Use backtracking as a means to travel to a new starting point. Vary your backtracking from close to loose following of the original stitching.

Backtracking

To define the term, backtracking is stitching over previous stitch lines, usually as a means of travel. There was a time when continuous line was the buzz and back-tracking was frowned upon in longarm quilting. As far as I'm concerned, that time has passed. I'm not suggesting that backtracking is always appropriate, but it has its place and certainly isn't taboo. In fact, it is now common to see beautiful quilting that incorporates intentional backtracking as an artistic technique. The very quilts that use backtracking can often be admired at national quilt shows, adorned with blue ribbons. This tells me that the technique is not only acceptable but pleasing to the judges when done well.

Remember, you are the artist; you compose the magic! You may have a quilt that lends itself to the dramatic enhancement of threads built up along the edges of a flower center or leaf vein. On the other hand, your vision might be one of a traditional design with repeated feathered motifs combined with intricate fillers. For this style, you may decide that backtracking should be minimal and concealed. If you prefer to minimize backtracking, you will want to create travel paths in your design process. A travel path can take the form of a double stem for a feather-like motif or any other space that can accept stitched additions that will be your transportation to a new starting point. Refer to Feathers and Fillers (page 49) for more information on creating and stitching along travel paths.

Practice backtracking with the following designs. I use this curlicue shape as the basis for many of my designs. It is versatile and fun to create. Notice the different effects that result from perfect and imperfect backtracking. There is not a right or a wrong way, just different. Remember, you are the executive decision maker; enjoy yourself!

This design successfully uses backtracking as an artistic tool.

This traditional quilting style is best stitched with minimal backtracking.

Speed

It is important to remember that your machine has many speeds, as do your movements. Familiarize yourself with the speed button because you will need to adjust the machine's speed often to perfect your freehand skills. If you prefer to use your machine in stitch-regulated mode, adjust the speed at which you move the machine. There are times to stitch slowly and times to speed up. Intricate designs requiring precise placement of stitches are nearly impossible to execute smoothly at a fast speed. You achieve much better control when moving slowly. As a general rule, the smaller the design, the slower the speed. However, if you are creating a loose, flowing, allover design, you can maneuver smoother curves at a quicker speed. Experiment with different speeds and design sizes on your practice pieces. Remember to make notes about your personal harmonic speeds.

Drag Bag

Ironically, too much freedom in your movement can hinder precise stitch placement. You can obtain better control by adding a bit of drag to your quilt. Initially, I added weight to my quilt in the form of cans of food. I found that this also helped to reduce the annoying vibration that was sometimes created at disharmonic speeds. This vibration kink seems to have been worked out, thankfully, in newer machines. However, the need for adding a bit of resistance remains. I add drag by using a heat pack intended for sore muscles. The bag is partially filled (about ⅔) with rice, so it adds the right amount of weight and is maneuverable. Attach the extended base to your machine to create a platform for the drag bag.

Create your own drag bag by sewing 2 pieces of fabric (approximately 5″ × 18″) together, leaving an opening at the top. Then fill it ⅔ of the way full with rice, beans, or similar weighted filler. Stitch the opening closed and you are ready to roll!

Attitude

A positive attitude will be reflected in your work. Have you ever heard of the little engine that could? You can! Set your expectations high, but allow yourself room for error. Expect improvement. I love to look back at some of my first quilts. They are just terrible, full of uneven stitches, jerky movements, and unbalanced spaces. I refer back to them on occasion and always smile when I do. They are proof that I have learned, grown, and improved my skills in a fairly short period. I accept my current level of skill, plan for improvement, and look forward to future works and growth.

Avoid comparing your work with that of other quilters. We each progress at a different rate. As you learn, remember that your only competitor is yourself. For most, longarm quilting begins as a hobby; for some, it progresses into a career. Hobby is the key word here. Hobbies are intended to provide pleasure and happiness. Approach your machine with a happy attitude, free from mental tension and stress, which will inevitably translate into your work. Look forward to your "play dates" with your machine!

Music

Music can be a powerful and emotionally uplifting tool. Try playing upbeat music in the background as you stitch. Select music according to the designs you plan to create. Funky, whimsical designs might be fun to stitch out while listening to a funky tune. There have been numerous studies about the relationship between classical music and learning. Classical music has been shown to enhance problem solving, improve focus, and increase concentration. So the next time you find yourself frustrated, struggling with a block to your creativity, perhaps Mozart can help!

Complementary, 63" × 63"

Feathers and Fillers

I must admit, I have quite a feather fetish. My life is simply better knowing that I coexist with such a lovely shape! Feathers have been around for ages; they are like the blue jeans of the quilting world—always in style. And you can dress them up or keep them casual. I've been told that some people have an aversion to feathers. If you're one of the few feather haters in existence, I'm not going to give up on you just yet. Read on, open your mind a bit, and let me see if I can convert you. I truly believe that there is a feather for every person, every style, maybe even every quilt. I am going to take you through the reasons that I love feathers, my techniques for drafting feathers, and my methods for stitching feathers.

Style

No two feathers are alike. They come in different shapes, sizes, and even styles. If you compare the feathered designs of two quilters, you will most likely see some differences. Perhaps one quilter has short, chunky feathers while the other has long, skinny feathers. They are both correct, just different based on the likes or dislikes of the executive decision maker, the quilter. Most people tend to have a natural feather style, although the ultimate factor for determining feather style should be the needs and style of the quilt. Examine the feathers shown at right. Which one are you most attracted to? Why? Identifying the reasons that you are drawn to a particular design will help you to develop your own style. Of course, you should not limit yourself or enter into a feather rut. Remember to determine the style and needs of the quilt in question first, and then plan your quilting designs accordingly.

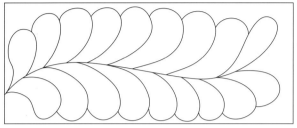

Traditional feather: Feathered designs like this one are usually connected to one another with minimal backtracking evidence. This style of feather lends itself well to repeated motif and border designs.

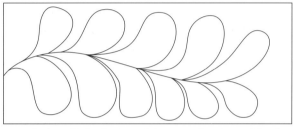

Curvy feather: This feather is much less tame than the traditional one. Its plumes are unconnected and it has more aggressive curves. This style of feather is great for freehand work and can easily be incorporated into an allover design.

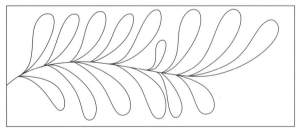

Folk art feather: This feather is elongated and much thinner than the other two. The plumes are unconnected and spaced far apart, cutting back on the need for backtracking. This style is perfect for quilts of a folk art or country style. It is a great choice for freehand border or sashing designs. This feather style also lends itself well to filling urn motifs, as discussed in Vases and Urns (page 25).

Feather Anatomy

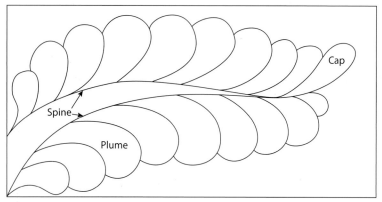

Feathers are composed of three elements: the spine, the plumes, and the cap.

Spine

The spine is the foundation that the feather plumes rest along. The spine can be a wavy line, a circle, or some other shape. It is merely the basis for the feather and is only limited by your imagination. Be creative with the spine design. A spine might be thick or thin, single or double, even or tapered—fashion it in whatever way you see fit! Double spines have the added benefit of providing a space to travel along when stitching, eliminating or reducing the amount of backtracking. Double spines can also present creative opportunities to include intricate details, such as circles, scallops, and loops, into your designs. Experiment!

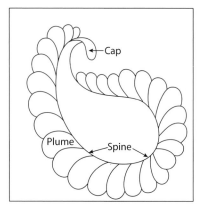

Spines are not limited to gradual curves or straight lines. They can come in various shapes, like this paisley.

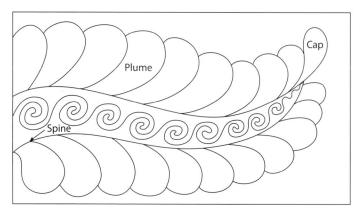

This doubled spine has created an open space that invites creative detail additions.

Plumes

The plumes are the shapes stacked along the spine to create the design. A traditional feather plume is shaped like half of a heart. However, the shape can be altered or enhanced to suit the mood of the quilt. Don't limit your feathered designs to use in feminine quilts. Feathers can play masculine roles as well.

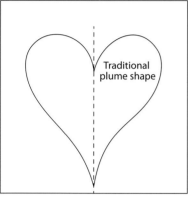

Draw a basic heart shape. Now divide it in half, and this is what a traditional feather plume resembles.

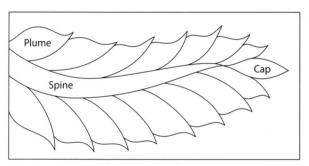

Changing the style of the plume from the traditional half heart to this organic, leaflike shape makes the feather take on a different feel. This feather style will perfectly accompany quilts with masculine themes, which sometimes present design challenges.

Cap

The cap of the feather is the stopping point or tip of the feathered design. It can be a basic teardrop or any variation thereof. Try exchanging the traditional teardrop feather cap for an element drawn from the quilt. For example, if the theme of the quilt is autumn, with leaves starring in the appliqué or fabric design, cap your feather with a leaf. The slightest changes sometimes produce the most dynamic impact. Study the quilt's contents for shape inspiration. The options for capping feathers are limitless.

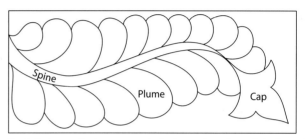

Don't limit your feather caps to the basic teardrop shape. Spice 'em up!

Feathers have been around for ages; they are like the blue jeans of the quilting world—always in style.

Feather Drafting

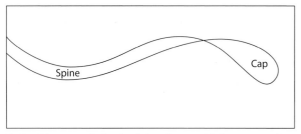

Begin with a capped-off spine. It is easiest to add plumes to a spine whose curves are gradual.

I always begin drawing my feathers at the base and work my way up. When drawing a traditional feather plume, mimic the shape of a half heart. Stack the plumes atop one another, keeping each plume's upper edge at a 45° angle to the stem. It is important that this angle remain consistent even as the spine shape shifts. Try reducing the size of the plumes as you progress up the spine to create a tapered effect.

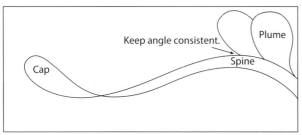

Pay close attention to the angle created by the upper edge of the plume and the spine. This angle should stay consistent as you work your way upward.

Aggressive Curves

Sometimes you may need to incorporate aggressive curves within your spine design. It might be your creative decision to do so or it might be necessary to fill empty space. When curves are sharp, it can be difficult to maintain the 45° angle between the plume's upper edge and the spine. The plumes may become misshapen, sometimes appearing fingerlike. To avoid creating finger feathers, introduce secondary shapes, such as curlicues, filigrees, and leaves. I consider these to be my "savior shapes." Not only will one of these shapes get you out of a bind, but it will add creative interest to your design. When I incorporate a secondary shape to save a feather, I often repeat the saving shape as the feather cap for unity.

As the spine's curve becomes drastic, the plumes have difficulty retaining the correct angle. They appear fingerlike.

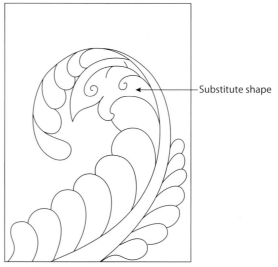

Avoid "finger plumes" by using a different shape, such as this filigree.

Branching Out

You can successfully fill your quilt's spaces with all the feathers you could hope for by branching off of one feather to create additional feathers. This technique is very simple and adds a bit of flair to your feather frenzy. This technique also lends itself beautifully to border design.

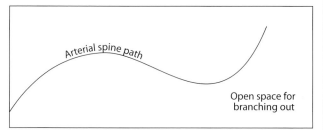

Begin the arterial spine path, leaving space for a new path to begin.

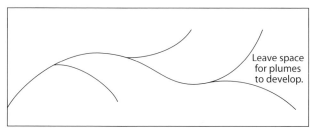

The two paths should diverge, forming a V shape, to allow adequate space for plume development.

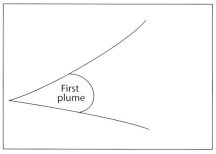

Place your first plume at the base of the V. It should be directionless, resembling a teardrop.

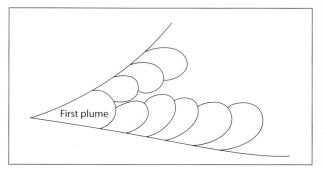

Complete the inner V by adding plumes to each separate side.

Stitching Paths

For most of my feather work, I like to reduce the amount of backtracking by creating stitching paths. Stitching paths provide a place for stitches to travel from one point to the next. Half of the traveling will take place on the outer edge of the plumes; the rest will take place at the spine. I like to incorporate space within the feather spine as room to travel. The traveling stitches are generally in the form of small, continuous filler designs or other small details that provide aesthetic as well as functional benefits. Study my stitching path below for the reduction of backtracking. Practice this stitching path using a pencil and paper until it feels comfortable to you, and then take the technique to the machine.

No-Backtrack Ornamental Feathers

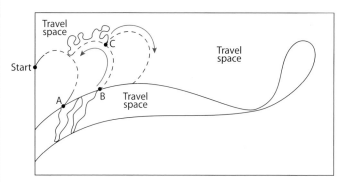

To stitch this feathered design with minimal or no backtracking, begin by stitching the feather cap and then stitching down the spine. Once you reach the bottom of the spine, you can begin stitching the plumes. Stitch the first plume, working from the outside in and ending at point A. You need to begin the second plume at point B, so travel along the spine using decorative wavy stitching in order to position the needle without backtracking. Create the second plume by stitching from the inside to the outside this time. Now you need to travel to point C to begin the third plume. Travel along the beginnings of your selected filler until you arrive at point C (see Fillers, page 54). Repeat until that entire side of the feather has been completed. To complete the plumes of the second side, position the needle at the base of the new side so that you can work upward, as shown in the illustration.

Single Spines

If the spine of the feather simply wants to be alone, don't fear. You can still stitch the design without backtracking. This technique excites me beyond belief! It eliminates the need for any backtracking while adorning the feather's upper edge beautifully. Incorporate these ornamental feathers in any of your feathered designs. To have some fun experimenting with possible variations, stitch them out easily and quickly as shown below:

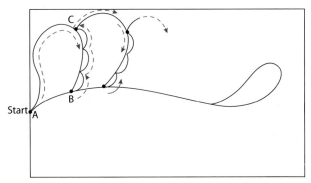

Begin with a basic feather design. Always stitch the cap first, then the spine, so that you have a place to add the plumes.

Start the plumes at the base of the design, point A. Stitch the first plume, working from the outside in. You are now at point B.

To get from point B (the stopping point of the first plume) to point C (the starting point for the next plume), create small scallop shapes along the upper edge of the first plume, stopping at point C.

Repeat until the first side is complete. Begin a new starting point for the second side so that you can work upward.

The possibilities for stylizing these backtrack-free ornamental feathers are endless. Have fun experimenting with your own one-of-a-kind details!

 TIP

Though these ornamental feathers can be stitched without marking, I like to premark them so that I have clear stop and start reference points. It is not necessary to mark the small details.

Fillers

Fillers are the small, continuous quilting designs used to fill in the empty spaces that surround motifs, border designs, appliqué, and other elements. The ultimate goal of the filler is to enhance the quilting designs, making them "pop." As the background recedes with the small filler stitches, the focal points appear bolder. While this portion of the quilting process can be relaxing and therapeutic, it can be intense if the chosen filler design is complex and intricate. Muscle aches are not uncommon during this portion of the quilting process.

Careful consideration should be given when planning out fillers. Remember—the size of your filler designs needs to remain consistent throughout to maintain balance. If you begin the journey with small, intricate stitching, you must be willing to go the distance. For example, if you include an abundance of micro-sized stippling in each of the blocks, be sure to extend a similar amount of quilting out to the borders. So be aware from the outset of the spaces that need fillers. If they are large and you have selected a small or complex filler design, plan for a healthy investment of time and energy.

Filler-to-Subject Size Contrast

It can be a bit of a challenge to determine the right amount of size variation to create between subject and filler. If the subject is a quilted motif or an appliqué design, there has to be a considerable scaling down of the filler designs so that the background can become flattened, exaggerating the "puff" of the subject. Otherwise, the filler designs merely blend into the subject and the spotlighting effect is lost. Before stitching your filler designs, audition several different sizes either on paper or directly on the quilt, alongside the subject, using an air-erasable marker.

Compare the following examples that show ineffective versus effective size contrast.

The scale of this stippling is much too large for this flower design. The shape of the flower becomes hidden by the stippling, which is too similar in scale.

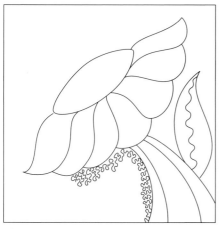

This stippling design is too intricate. It causes the petals to appear wrinkly in comparison.

This is the right scale. It provides the right amount of dimension to enhance—not hide—the design.

 TIP

I love to listen to audio books while I stitch my filler designs. I find that most fillers are repetitive, involving less concentration than other quilting designs. I always reserve audio book listening for machine time and look forward to my visits with my favorite authors. Sometimes I find myself quilting for an hour or two extra because I can't bear to put the book down, so to speak. It is easy to lose motivation during this sometimes monotonous process. Audio books can hold your interest and keep your mind alert. In addition, audio books can help you track your quilting time. I keep a stack of the books I have finished during a particular project and then add up the hours listed on each box. I am always surprised at the significant time investment I have made.

Speed

Remember to stitch slowly so you can remain in control. It is much easier to execute intricate designs when stitching or moving the machine slowly. If you have a stitch regulator, try turning it off and using manual mode. This may be necessary to achieve the smaller stitch length necessary to quilt successful small shapes. For example, at ten stitches per inch, tiny circles will look like tiny squares.

Design Variety

Though using just one style of filler throughout your quilt can unify the piece, at times it can become monotonous. If you like variety or become bored easily, try incorporating many different filler styles into your quilt. Most quilts have natural breaks, such as seams, inner and outer motif portions, and so on. These breaks are the perfect place to integrate new designs. But remember to keep the density consistent from one filler to the next.

Thread

Filler quilting is small in scale; the stitches lie close together. If you don't want your designs to become enveloped by thread, select a fine thread weight. When stitching fillers, I don't use threads heavier than 50 weight for basic designs, such as stippling. For complex filler designs, I always use the finest thread available—100 weight.

Sample Designs

These are some of the fillers I often use in my quilting. Any of them can be translated into allover designs, taking the place of a pantograph if you prefer working from the front of the machine. Simply make the design larger and more open. Experiment with size variations for different effects. Trace the design with your fingertips until you understand its flow and direction, and then take it to your next quilt!

Stippling

Stippling has existed for ages. There has been mention of its overuse, but I still enjoy it and consider it my loyal filler friend. I find it to be extremely relaxing to stitch and appropriate for countless styles beyond just traditional. Stippling supports a subject, allowing the subject to perform its starring role. If stippling were an ice cream flavor, it would be vanilla. Not overpowering, just pleasant.

When stippling, avoid patterned stitching by changing direction regularly.

Wiggle Worms

I call this design "wiggle worms" because the curvy, bent shapes remind me of the little earthworms I encounter in my garden. They poke their little heads up and then wiggle back into the earth. I started using this design as stipple relief. I wanted a more original design with the same neutral qualities as stippling.

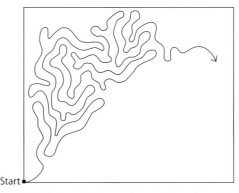

Begin this design with the earthworm shapes branching out in opposite directions. Echo around, creating new worms often.

Cumulus

Inspired by clouds, these whimsical shapes are cheerful and will add life to your quilting projects.

Create clouds in random shapes, backtracking at the curls for added dimension and as a means to travel to a new starting point for the next shape. Overlapping and partial shapes add interest and enable you to avoid frequent starts and stops.

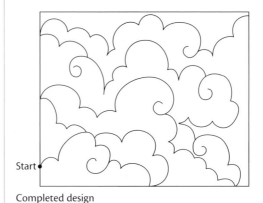

Completed design

Sweethearts

These hearts get their charm from their irregularity. They add a unique element to your quilting while quickly filling in empty spaces.

Begin with a whimsical heart shape, the more unusual the better, and then add new but similar heart shapes, changing direction, shape, and size as you quilt along. Create dimension and flair by adding partial shapes with wild, elongated curves. You will need to step out of the box for this one!

Candlelight

This filler is a great choice for intricate show quilting. It creates a beautiful texture, especially when small in scale.

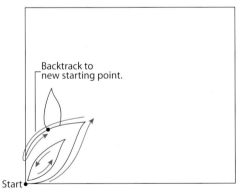

Begin with a leaflike shape. Echo the initial shape one or more times and then travel along your stitch line to a new starting point. Repeat. For added interest, vary the direction of the shapes and the frequency of the echoes.

Start
Completed design

Curlicues

This design is extremely versatile and open to customization. It is fairly simple to master. It involves a great deal of back-tracking, which adds character when done imperfectly. This design looks beautiful stitched densely for filler or loosely as an allover design. Additional elements, such as leaves, flowers, and butterflies, can be added easily.

Start

To create this design, begin with a curlicue shape. Backtrack from its point outward until you reach a new starting point. Avoid patterns, alternating the curls from one direction to the other.

Raspberry Truffle, 72" × 72"

To Mark or Not to Mark

If you desire a completely uniform look with repeated designs, identical from one space to another, it will be necessary to mark them on your quilt. I prefer to mark the majority of my quilting designs before quilting, especially for custom and show quilt applications. I find the end result is well worth the preparation time. Once the design and drafting work is in the rearview mirror, it's just you and the open road!

Marking Implements

Many different marking implements are available to quilters. Here are a few of my favorites—and a few factors to consider when selecting the right tool for the job.

 TIP

You should always perform a test using the exact marking implement combined with the exact fabric you plan to mark. You want to be confident that the marks are completely removable and will not remain in your work once you are finished.

Water-Soluble Pen

Water-soluble pens are a great choice for many reasons: They are visible on most fabric shades, the markings remain until you remove them with water, and they transfer easily. If you plan to use water-soluble pens for marking, you want to be confident that the quilt fabrics will not bleed when you remove the markings. These marks usually require a thorough soaking for adequate removal. You might even notice mark or color reappearance, which will require additional wetting.

Some quilters opt not to prewash their fabrics. If you are among them or are unsure if the fabrics have been prewashed, test them for bleeding. Hand-dyed fabrics are particularly prone to bleeding. To test, soak the fabric in question with water and then sandwich it between two

white fabrics or paper towels. Press with a hot iron. Check the white fabrics for dye transfer. If they are still white, you can be confident that future bleeding will not occur.

My preferred, tried-and-true water-soluble pen

Air-Erasable Pen

These pens are an excellent choice when you plan to finish your quilting job soon. Their marks disappear without the use of water, so they are safe to use on fabrics that are prone to dye transfer. However, you need to be aware of your time frame and the weather when using these pens. Depending on the humidity in the air, the marks can last for several days or just several hours.

Air-erasable pen marks disappear on their own. Make sure you have time to quilt before the marks vanish!

Marking Pencil

Sewline ceramic-lead mechanical pencils provide a fine line that transfers smoothly to the fabric and is especially visible on dark fabrics. I prefer mechanical pencils because they eliminate the need for and mess of sharpeners. You will find that once the lines have been quilted over and your quilt rolled and manipulated, most of the lines will have disappeared. If any marking lines are still visible, simply rub them away using a dry cloth or toothbrush.

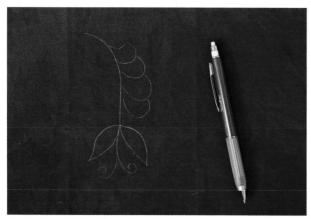

The Sewline ceramic lead produces a fine line that is easy to follow.

 TIP

During the marking process, make sure that only your erasable marking implement is near your work space. It would be disastrous if you accidentally grabbed your design-drafting permanent Sharpie and proceeded to mark the quilt with it. If you're anything like me, you get so excited when it's almost time to quilt that your brain turns to mush! It's always best to be a defensive quilter on the lookout for possible catastrophes!

Preload Marking

A lightbox is a great way to mark designs on your quilt top before loading it onto the longarm machine. If you don't have a lightbox, refer to Creating a Lightbox (page 23) for how to make one. I find that this do-it-yourself lightbox provides sufficient light even for black fabric. If you have trouble seeing the design through dark or patterned fabric, elevate the light source so it is closer to your design.

NOTE

Preload tasks are done on the quilt top prior to loading it onto the longarm machine with the batting and backing.

Postload tasks are done on the quilt, batting, and backing trio that is already pinned onto the longarm machine.

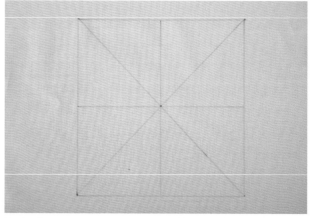

Mark reference points: centers, sectioned lines, and so on.

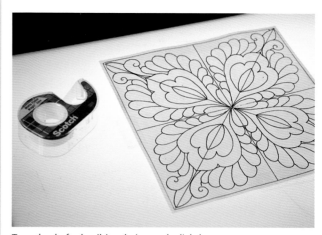

Tape the drafted quilting design to the lightbox.

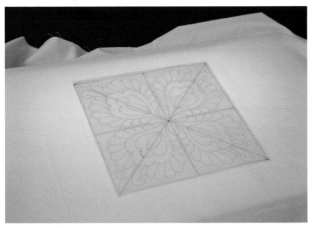

Position the quilt over the drafted design, lining up the reference points.

To prevent the quilt from slipping or shifting as you mark, place several beanbags or cans of food on top of the quilt.

Transfer the design to your quilt. Turn off the light periodically to check for adequate marking.

Postload Marking

There may be times when you have already loaded your quilt onto the machine and begun quilting, and then decide to add a block motif that you plan to repeat throughout. Last-minute creative moments often present themselves as you are immersed in the quilting process. Also, you will sometimes want to mimic an appliqué or fabric design element within the quilting. At this point it is too late to mark the designs using a light table because the three layers are secured and would prevent the light from shining through. In this situation, use the postload method (I use it often).

I like to use Solvy for the postload marking technique. Solvy is a water-soluble stabilizer that is transparent and flexible, sometimes used for thread play and lacemaking. I always keep several rolls on hand. It should be stored in an airtight container or ziplock bag because it can lose its pliability when left out too long.

1. Mark your quilting design and reference points onto the Solvy using an erasable marking pen. It is very important that you don't use permanent ink, which can become stitched into the fiber, permanently discoloring your quilt.

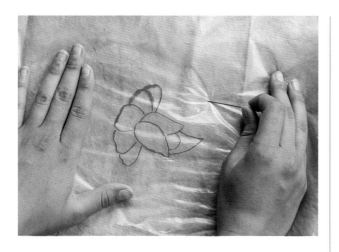

2. When you are ready to quilt, pin the marked Solvy onto your quilt, matching the reference points.

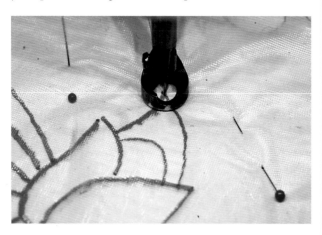

3. Stitch the design right through the Solvy.

4. Gently tear away the Solvy. Use a pin to lift the Solvy away from inner shapes. Usually the stabilizer tears away completely. If some Solvy remains in your stitching, simply spritz it with water and it will dissolve, never to be seen or heard from again!

Partial Marking

Partial marking done loosely can be a great benefit for free-hand work. By marking reference points and sectioning off spaces, you can make your freehand quilting appear more uniform. Partial marking can be done pre- or postload. If you plan to section off spaces postload, use a flexible ruler, which will bend with the slack in the quilt.

 TIP

For quick and easy block motifs, you can mark the block skeleton shapes that you have created using template plastic (page 27). When I quilt with block skeletons, I simply mark as I go, one block at a time, using self-made templates. This way, I can use an air-erasable marking implement, eliminating the extra step of mark removal. It is not necessary to mark any details; those can be added freehand as you stitch.

Wolf Impressions, 24" × 32"

Rulers and Gridwork

Rulerwork refers to quilting straight lines using a ruler to guide you along a straight path. Longarm rulers are approximately ¼″ thick so that they will not slip under the hopping foot of the longarm machine. An extended base is added to the machine to provide a platform on which the ruler rests.

As a new longarm quilter, I avoided rulerwork like it was the flu! The thought of quilting straight lines on a machine that moves so freely just seemed unnatural. I believed that if I simply didn't own a ruler, the need for it would never arise. I soon discovered that I was wrong. Each and every quilt is unique. Some quilts are content with an allover freehand design holding them together. Others, "high-maintenance quilts," as I like to refer to them, demand more love and labor from the quilter.

Having rulerwork skills in your arsenal of mastered techniques will place you in high demand if you quilt for others. Versatility is a useful thing in longarm quilting. Consider rulerwork the next fun challenge in the journey toward longarm artistry.

Extended Base

You will need to attach a base to your machine, which will serve as a platform for the ruler. Most machine purchases include a ruler base as a provided attachment. If you don't own a base, I would recommend investing in one either directly from your machine's manufacturer or from a secondary source. It is important that the base be attached to the machine properly. It should present a flat, stable surface for you to work on. If the base is attached with screws, check them often. Sometimes screws work their way loose, resulting in a wobbly base. Some ruler bases extend beyond the front edge of the machine, cutting your work space short. Familiarize yourself with the new travel limitations so you can anticipate the stopping point. Otherwise you might unexpectedly crash into the bar, messing up your stitch flow.

An extended base should be attached to your machine firmly when you are using a straight-line guide.

Rulers for Straight Lines

There is no shortage of straight-line guides available to quilters. I tend to be a bit of a minimalist in terms of tools, relying on practice and ability instead. You really only need one ruler to assist you in your straight work. My personal preference is a handle-free ruler with ¼″ markings. I like to use a manageable size, no larger than 2″ × 12″. I prefer no handle because I maneuver the ruler as I stitch along to stay on a straight path. I am right-handed, so I use my right hand to control the machine and my left to guide the ruler. I keep a wide stance, so to speak, with my left hand. This gives me a wider range of motion for the slight ruler shifting that takes place. If you are left-handed, simply reverse the stance.

My preferred straight-line guide

Here are my stances for vertical or diagonal and for horizontal rulerwork. At first these may seem a bit awkward, but you will quickly gain confidence and comfort with a bit of practice.

Vertical or Diagonal Lines

Your thumb, index, and middle fingers are the key players in vertical and diagonal lines. Your middle finger acts as an anchor, providing stability to the ruler, which rests along that finger. This anchoring finger is very important. It prevents the machine from pushing the ruler off track. Your thumb and index finger do the driving. They perform the necessary subtle movements to keep your stitching along its path.

Stance for vertical or diagonal lines

Horizontal Lines

For horizontal lines, the key players change a bit: Your thumb stays in the game, with your pinky and ring fingers joining. This time, the pinky is the anchor; the thumb and ring finger control the movements.

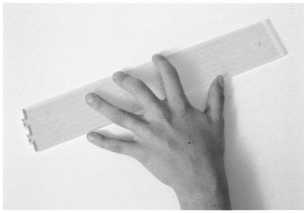

Stance for horizontal lines

 TIP

Avoid distributing weight to the edge of the ruler that is away from the needle. Applying weight to this edge may result in a tip of the ruler. If the ruler tips upward, the hopping foot can slip under the ruler and you risk sewing onto the ruler. Not only will this cause a needle break, but it may result in damage to your machine.

PRACTICE EXERCISE

The best practice doesn't necessarily need to take place at the machine. You can familiarize yourself with rulers when you're away from the machine—watching TV, waiting for water to boil, and so on. Here is a great exercise to help you begin gaining confidence with ruler maneuvers. Pay close attention to your finger position on the ruler.

1. Draw several straight, connecting lines on a piece of paper, changing direction and angle often for extra practice.

2. Secure the marked paper to a counter or tabletop.

3. Tape a marker, in a contrasting color to the paper marks, to the side of a book. Be sure to use plenty of tape so that the marker is attached firmly.

4. Imagine the marker is the needle and the marked paper is a quilt. With the marker leaning on the edge of the ruler for support and guidance, trace over the paper marks in swift, smooth movements.

Stitch in-the-Ditch

Stitch in-the-ditch (SID) is a method for anchoring the seamlines of your quilt and providing stability to the overall piece. It involves stitching right in the "ditch" between two pieced elements, where the quilting will become concealed within the seam line. This standard technique can be simplified with the assistance of a ruler. Though I have heard of some who have mastered it freehand, I have come to rely on the support of my ruler, which I find reduces undesired stitch wobbling.

When a pieced quilt calls for custom work, you will want to incorporate SID. The patterns and designs created by pieced blocks, sashing, and borders truly come alive when the seams are stitched down. Longarm SID is definitely more difficult and time-consuming than domestic-machine SID. Be patient with yourself and accept that a lot of practice will be necessary to master this technique.

In addition to practice, well-pressed seams and accurate piecing provide the best foundation for SID. The fact that fabric is easily manipulated can be both a blessing and a curse. For example, a perfectly straight seam can become distorted by weight or pressure. On the other hand, imperfect seams can become straighter with some manipulation and guidance.

Generally, SID should be performed at a slow speed. It is easier to remain in the ditch when you are in control. In addition, pieced blocks usually present many shifts in direction. It is usually necessary to stop the machine at each directional change so that you can adjust the ruler accordingly.

Crosshatching

Gridwork on a longarm machine is revered by some and feared by many. If you suffer from "crosshatchophobia," as I once did, now is the time to overcome your fears! It is with good reason that crosshatching has carried on through the centuries with timeless appeal. Its simplicity is highly effective and wonderfully versatile.

Crosshatching, like other forms of straight quilting, is most successful when combined with curved shapes, such as feathered or floral motifs. It is also a fitting solution for busy appliqué quilts in which the appliqué designs play the starring role. In such cases, selecting quilting designs too similar in shape and style to the appliqués themselves may result in detraction from both. The eye becomes overstimulated, in need of a resting place. Crosshatching can play the role of the neutral ally. The contrasting combination of simplicity and complexity provides beauty and balance, drawing the eye to the quilt's focal points.

The Case for Marking

I might be a bit old-fashioned in my crosshatching technique, selecting the long route, but the positive results are consistent. I mark my lines ahead of time. Yes, each and every one. Believe it or not, it's not as time consuming as you might think. Why do I mark my lines, especially considering all of the tools available for crosshatching that promise to do the job faster than marking? Here are a few reasons I mark:

- Customizable spacing and sizing, not predetermined

- Strategic line placement

- Easy variability

Marked lines provide a constant guide. Relying on the edge of a ruler as your sole guide (common in nonmarking techniques) may result in inconsistencies. The angle may begin to shift slightly with each added line. After many inches have been quilted, the imperfection becomes obvious, and by then it can be hard to correct.

The grid lines for crosshatching can be marked either pre- or postload. If I am using crosshatching in small doses, such as in motif or appliqué details, I will mark them postload using a flexible ruler. For more extensive crosshatching, it is a good idea to mark the quilt prior to loading it. Preload marking will allow you to work on a flat surface. A flat surface will assist you in creating clean, straight lines, free of distortion.

Begin by selecting an angle and a stitch pattern. Traditional crosshatching involves a 45° angle in both directions, with single, evenly spaced stitch lines. But there are many variations on this traditional design that may be more suitable for the mood of your quilt. You may wish to vary the angles to produce diamondlike crosshatching or alternate the thread colors to produce specific effects. I created a plaid-like effect in a portion of my quilt *Ambrosia* (page 70) by alternating thread colors and varying the widths of the lines, as shown below. For this application, I marked the lines postload using a flexible ruler.

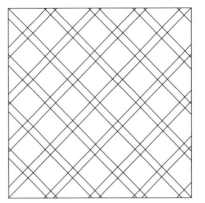

Double-lined crosshatching with varied widths

Plaid effect

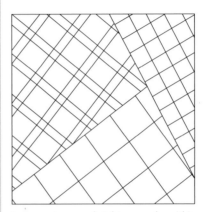

Incorporate a crosshatching sampler within your space for a unique patchwork effect.

Once you have decided on a plan of attack, you are ready to begin marking. I like to place my first marked line at the center point and work outward. In some instances, such as alongside a shape, it may be necessary to provide yourself with a straight line as a guide for the angle. This is demonstrated in the inner portion of this feathered design.

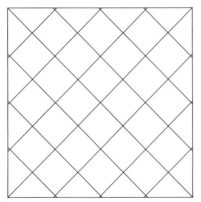

Traditional crosshatching—45° angle with single lines

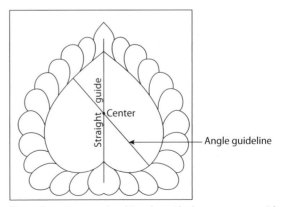

If you plan to use crosshatching alongside shapes, you may wish to temporarily add a straight line as a guide for selecting the correct angle when marking your lines. In addition, mark the center of the shape for an evenly spaced grid.

Stitching Crosshatching

I thoroughly enjoy stitching out crosshatched patterns.

I find it to be a soothing quilting technique. With some confidence and practice, you will too. To stitch the numerous repeated straight lines, you need either some travel space or some time and patience for frequent stops and starts. A combination of the two is a good compromise.

When stitching the marked cross-hatched lines, avoid stitching them consecutively. Instead, stitch every third or fourth row and then return later to complete the stitching. This will create stability, preventing distortion. You can plan travel paths into the design to reduce backtracking and stops and starts (page 86). You can opt to travel along the seam's ditches when needed, as long as you have selected an unobtrusive thread. If you have selected a heavyweight thread, which will appear built up when back-tracked, it might be necessary to clip or bury the threads (page 87) with each new line.

 TIP

Small doses of crosshatching can have a big impact. Enhance inner portions of block motifs or appliqué designs with small-scale crosshatching to create variety and capture the eye.

Grids as Guides for Freehand Work

Marking grids to accommodate freehand work can be very effective. The grid markings can serve as reference points, creating uniformity in your freehand designs. Your eyes will be grateful that you provided them with the groundwork.

Continuous Curve

This impressive continuous design can be completed with just one start and stop. I have heard it referred to as "wineglass," "orange peel," and "pumpkin seeds." Call it whatever you'd like; it's beautiful and versatile. It can be created using the seams of your patchwork as reference points, or you can create your own grid marks using a ruler and an erasable marking implement. Though it appears complex, with the right machine speed selected, it is fairly simple to create. If you are beginning with a small grid, such as ½″ squares, stitch very slowly to remain in control. If your grid is larger, 1″ or more, then you should stitch slightly faster. Remember, if you feel out of control, slow down.

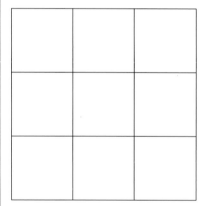

Begin with an even grid, either created by the seams of your patchwork or marked with an erasable marking implement.

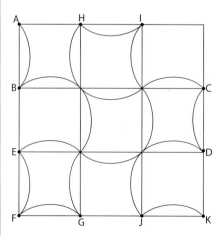

I usually begin stitching this continuous design at the corner. Follow the letters to learn the path to follow.

1. Stitch down from A to B with a scallop shape.

2. Create a serpentine shape, shifting the curves at the intersecting lines of the grid until you reach C.

3. Next, drop down to D and then serpentine over to E.

4. Create the corner by scalloping over to F, then G.

5. Now it is time to begin the upward serpentine shapes. Continue stitching in alphabetical order until you reach K.

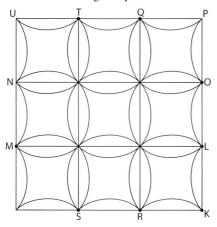

1. To complete the second half of the stitching, begin where you left off at K. Scallop up from K to L.

2. Now serpentine over to M. (Half of the serpentine shape is already stitched, so stitch along the opposite sides.)

3. Scallop up to N, and then serpentine over to O.

4. Create the corner by scalloping up to P, then over to Q.

5. Serpentine down to R and then scallop over to S. Serpentine up to T and then scallop over to U.

You are finished, with a single stop and start!

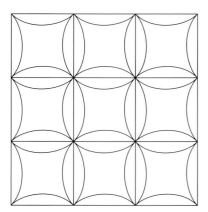

Uniform Scallops

I love the intricate look of rows of scalloped quilting. I like my scallops to be uniform in size. This can be easily achieved by marking a grid to use as a reference, as shown in these examples.

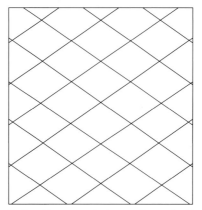

Begin with a premarked, even diamond grid.

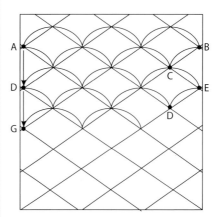

The scallop shapes are stitched in rows, alternating from left to right. The valleys of the scallops in the first row line up with the peaks of the scallops in the row beneath it. Examine the stitch path until you understand the pattern, and then practice drawing and stitching the design.

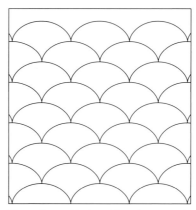

The scallops with the grid marks removed

Ambrosia, 90″ × 90″

Gotta Love Thread

So now that you are convinced that we quilters are indeed artists, let's talk about our medium of choice—thread! Thread is what we use to accomplish our artistic endeavors. Threads are like pairs of shoes—you can never have too many! I thoroughly enjoy collecting threads, admiring them, sharing them with others, and on occasion … using them! Have you ever been told or assumed that there were limitations to the types of thread you could use on your longarm machine? Guess what. It's simply not true; it's merely a myth. You can use any thread your little heart desires in that machine of yours. Now, that doesn't mean that all threads should be treated equally, but with a bit of education and patience you can use any thread you choose.

Popular Choices

Monofilament

I have been using monofilament thread since day one. I love it! I especially love it when it is time to stitch in-the-ditch (page 66) or outline appliqué. In these techniques, monofilament forgives the occasional wobble, rendering mistakes wonderfully unobtrusive. Monofilament is also an excellent choice for high-contrast areas. Let's face it—rethreading and preparing the machine for new thread takes some time. If I simply lack the time for thread-change preparation, I use monofilament. I find that it takes on the appearance of the fabric it rests upon, giving the impression that numerous thread colors were used.

Nylon Monofilament

This is my personal preference. My favorite brand of monofilament thread is Sew-Art. It lacks the shine produced by some polyester monofilaments. Its texture is similar to that of hair. It is extremely fine and possesses the right amount of strength. A thread's strength is important, but you shouldn't be able to cut through steel with it. I like to avoid the wiry monofilament threads that are like fishing line. To me, they just don't feel like thread. Quilting is a tactile medium, so all of the products used to create a quilt should have a soft touch.

Polyester Monofilament

Polyester is another great choice for monofilament thread. MonoPoly by Superior Threads is a great product, especially when a bit of shine or reflection is desired. I have found it to be extremely user-friendly with low breakage. Polyester monofilament is said to be more heat resistant than nylon. So if you plan to apply high heat directly to the thread, you might opt for polyester.

Clear or Smoke

Most monofilament threads are available in two colors, clear and smoke. I like to keep both colors on hand. Clear is meant to be used with light- to medium-colored fabrics, while smoke blends better when quilting darker fabrics.

Cotton

Cotton is a versatile natural fiber. Cotton thread offers a soft hand and is a perfect choice for those who prefer a matte finish. Look for high-quality cotton threads that are uniform in thickness, containing 100 percent long-staple fibers. If a bit of luster is desired, select mercerized cotton threads, which also produce less lint, keeping your machine cleaner. Typically, cotton threads are not completely colorfast, so bleach should be avoided when laundering.

Polyester

Polyester is a synthetic fiber that produces a very strong, durable thread. Spun polyester is a great choice if you desire the matte look of cotton with added strength and colorfastness. Trilobal polyester produces a beautiful sheen, comparable to the look of rayon. It is available in a vast array of solid and variegated colors, making it a great choice for decorative applications. Trilobal polyester is not as strong as other thread types. So if you plan to quilt at the speed of light, it probably won't cooperate. If its appearance has won you over, simply plan to slow down considerably while using it. As a compromise, alternate strong threads with decorative ones. Highlight decorative threads in vital spaces and fill areas that play more of a supporting role using stronger threads.

Polyester threads come in a large array, from decorative to utilitarian.

Silk

I like to refer to silk thread as the Cadillac of threads. It is high in quality, with an unrivaled luster combined with strength and durability. It is available in very fine weights, which is the reason I use it almost exclusively in show quilts. One drawback to using silk thread is its cost. It is significantly more expensive than most other thread types and can turn into quite an investment. For this reason, I don't keep silk threads in my stash. Rather, I purchase only what is needed to complete a given piece. In my opinion, however, its beauty outweighs its high price tag.

Silk threads provide a beautiful luster and are available in ultrafine weights.

Metallic

Metallic threads add a unique sparkle to quilting designs, reflecting light beautifully. They can absolutely be used in a longarm machine with proper treatment and care. Metallics are available in many different varieties and colors. Seek high-quality metallic threads, with a nylon core for added strength and an outer coating that protects the thread from shredding as you stitch. Metallic threads demand delicate treatment in exchange for their dazzling display. Most metallics won't tolerate Mach-speed quilting. Allow extra time when planning to use them. Using small amounts of metallic thread can be a great compromise, adding just enough shine without the time commitment.

Metallic threads add a touch of glitz to your quilting.

Color Selection

Don't judge a thread's color by the way it appears on the spool. To determine the right thread color, pull several inches of thread away from the spool and lay the strands over your work. If you plan to quilt using straight lines, position the thread in a straight line. Otherwise, scrunch it up over the quilt top. Consider your planned quilting density when selecting a color. Heavy quilting will obviously use more thread, resulting in a more significant color impact. Audition several possibilities—you may be surprised which thread color wins out.

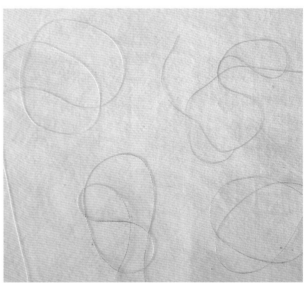

Audition thread colors by positioning several options atop your quilt.

Blended Color

Blending the thread color with that of the fabric will yield a textured result. If you are a beginner, this might be the best option because blended colors are more forgiving than contrasting ones.

Blending the thread color with the background can conceal imperfections.

Contrasting Color

Your quilting designs can really be spotlighted when you use a thread color that contrasts with that of the fabric. You may choose to match the hue but vary the shade considerably to create a shadowed or highlighted effect. Varying the colors altogether can be a great choice, especially to unify colors floating about the body of the quilt. If you plan to use contrasting threads, select quilting designs that you are confident stitching out to avoid stress. Mistakes will be much more evident with contrasting thread.

Contrasting threads produce dramatic results but are less forgiving of mistakes.

Variegated Colors

Variegated threads can add wonderful artistic effects. Some are single-color shade variegations while others contain a multitude of colors, shifting from one to the next. Multicolored variegated threads are a great way to unite all of the colors used throughout the body of a quilt. Single-colored thread variegations can be used to bring natural, earthy subjects to life through shadows and highlights. When choosing a variegated thread for your project, lay the complete variegation series over your fabric. Be aware of color shifts that are too similar to your fabric color. If sections of the variegated thread match the fabric too closely, the stitching will disappear briefly, creating breaks in the flow of your designs.

Avoid using variegated threads containing colors that match the fabric too closely.

 TIP

Thread color can be an important tool for densely quilted applications in which the thread plays a key role. The color temperature of the entire quilt can be altered by the choice of thread color. For example, if you want to warm up the appearance of a quilt, select threads of a warmer shade than that of the fabric. In my quilt *Ambrosia* (page 70), I felt that the rust-colored fabric was too dominantly orange, so I calmed it down using a subtle brown thread. In the example below, compare the fabric pre- and postquilting to see the difference made by the thread. Adjustments can also be made to change the quilt's shade by selecting lighter or darker threads according to your needs.

Rust-colored fabric prequilting—too orange

Postquilted fabric—toned down by warmer thread color choice

Weight

Weight should be central to your thread selection process. The smaller the weight number, the thicker the thread. For example, a 30-weight thread will be much heavier than a 100-weight thread, which is extremely fine. A thread's weight will have a great effect on the visual outcome of your work. Let's compare two extremes: 30 weight and 100 weight.

The dramatic flowers in *Complementary* were created with 30-weight thread.

Heavy: 30 Weight

A very heavy thread, 30-weight thread marks the limit of successful top use for most machines. Beyond 30 weight, the thread simply won't fit through the eye of the needle. This weight is an excellent choice for open designs in which the thread itself plays an integral role. It provides quick coverage while making a bold statement. This thread can beautifully showcase open crosshatching or other grid designs. In my show quilt *Complementary* (page 48), I used 30-weight silk thread to draw attention to the whimsical flower designs scattered about the border. As with everything, there is a time and a place for heavy thread. It is not usually a good choice for intricate motifs or fillers; it can overcrowd small-scale designs. It doesn't bury into the fabric the way finer threads do, so it can appear built up when backtracked. I think of heavy threads as limelight hoarders, so I use them in small doses.

TIP

For camouflaging less-than-perfect points, 30-weight thread is a great tool. Quilting an allover design works best. Just meander along, cleverly placing your stitches where the pieced point should be. The heavy stitch line conceals the imperfection perfectly.

Fine: 100 Weight

The day my longarm machine met 100-weight thread was the day my life changed. As an infant longarmer, I assumed that large cones of 40-weight polyester thread were my machine's preference. Curiosity took over, though, and I discovered that my machine is unbiased, enjoying diversity in its thread friends, playing well with most. What an enlightening day! I learned that intricate, heirloom-style quilting was attainable when combining this fine thread with my longarm machine. Talk about the best of both worlds! Extremely fine, 100-weight thread makes backtracked stitching undetectable. It is a great choice for intricate motifs and tedious filler work that requires close stitching. The thread buries into the fabric beautifully so that the quilting design, not the thread, is the star of the show. This thread is not the best choice for loose, open designs because its stitches may disappear altogether within the loft of the batting.

Fine thread, such as 100 weight, is a great choice for intricate quilting.

Successful Thread Use and Troubleshooting

Thread Path

The journey from spool to needle can be an arduous one for our much-loved threads. It is very important that you observe the thread's path closely. Slippery, decorative threads can easily become twisted and slip out of the tension discs. The thread's course is often overlooked as a contributor to thread breakage, resulting in multiple changes and adjustments that may present new problems. With each thread change, pull the thread slowly, releasing several inches from the spool. Examine the way it travels through the guides and tension discs to ensure an obstacle-free journey. Recheck this path often for slips and twists.

Thread Stance

It has been said that threads like to leave the spool according to the method in which they are wound—parallel, crosswound, and so on. However, I have had the greatest success by positioning my thread spools on their bases, so that the thread leaves its spool heading upward as shown on page 77.

Depending on your machine, it may be necessary to modify its thread holder. Some longarm machines are designed to hold only large cones of thread, not small spools, in this upright position. Smaller spool holders are often limited to a horizontal position at the top of the machine. You can affix an appropriate thread stand, which will accommodate smaller spools, to your machine using plumber's putty or similar products.

Don't be afraid to alter this aspect of your machine. You will be pleased with the new thread possibilities open to you, and you can always return your machine to its original setup. When I make modifications, I always take photographs of the original state for an easy return, if desired.

I have the most success when my threads dispense upward.

 TIP

One possible cause for thread breakage is when excess thread makes its way under the base of the spool and becomes wrapped around the spool holder. Thread flow is halted, and the result is broken thread. I like to offer my thread a bit of cushion where the excess thread can puddle gently. For pronged thread holders, cut out two circles approximately 4″ in diameter, one of cardboard and the other of batting. Create center notches in both circles and place them over the thread holder—they should rest on top of the prongs. The thread spool or cone rests atop the batting. For thread holders that have a flat base, omit the cardboard circle.

Create a soft cushion where thread can puddle gently as opposed to becoming wrapped around the spool holder.

 TIP

Slow the flow of thread by placing a snug net over the thread spool. This allows the thread to release in a slow, controlled manner. It often reduces tangling and prevents thread from slipping out of the tension discs, both of which can create problems. Floral nets are perfect for this application and are usually discarded weekly by florists, who will be happy to have you take them off their hands.

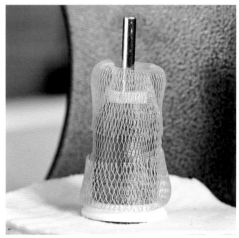

Control the flow of your thread by positioning a floral net over the spool.

Bobbin Thread

When I began longarm quilting, I believed that top and bobbin thread should be identical. That is, the bobbin should be wound from the exact spool that I planned to use on top. Then along came The Bottom Line by Superior Threads. It hadn't occurred to me that you could use different threads in the bobbin and on top. I used it once and thought, "Wow"; twice, "Wow" again; a third time, "Even better." I fell in love with this product. It was simply magic, obviously sent to me by some angel of threads. Not only did I love it, but my decorative threads blissfully concurred. Its smooth, fine texture lubricates the top threads, reducing breakage while producing a beautiful stitch.

I highly recommend this thread and have discovered that when I use it, it's not necessary to match top and bobbin colors exactly. Rather, I keep a supply of several large cones in light gray, medium gray, off-white, tan, medium brown, taupe, and black. These colors accommodate and blend nicely with just about any color. Colors from the blue and purple families will blend perfectly with the grays; greens, reds, and golds blend with the tan or brown; and so on. As an added benefit, the thread's fineness (60 weight) means that the bobbin will hold considerably more yardage than it would of a heavier thread. Fewer bobbin changes means more uninterrupted quilting progress!

Don't underestimate the power of the bobbin.

Prewound Bobbins

I was recently introduced to another fantastic product that I highly recommend. Fil-Tec has produced a prewound bobbin called Magna-Glide. Before I found this product, I felt that prewound bobbins were inferior to ones I wound myself. It seemed as though the tension in a prewound bobbin was affected as the amount of thread dwindled. This is not true with Magna-Glide bobbins. The thread on these bobbins is fantastic to use; it is a fine (60-weight) polyester with a smooth surface texture that lubricates delicate, temperamental upper threads nicely. Breakage—nearly nil. Headaches—not anymore! But the true beauty of these little round wonders is in their system of delivery. The bobbin core is magnetic, eliminating the need for a backlash spring. Overspinning is managed by the magnet instead. I have found that it always delivers a beautiful stitch to the last drop of thread.

Understanding Tension

Never rely on your machine's factory settings to determine the proper amount of tension. You should feel comfortable making adjustments to the tension of both the top and bobbin thread on a daily basis. The only right setting is the one that produces a pretty stitch, and the only wrong setting is the one that produces an ugly stitch.

How do you differentiate pretty stitches from ugly ones? Pretty stitches have the right amount of tension balance, top and bottom. They should look and feel nice, burying into the fabric well. You shouldn't see or feel traces of the bobbin thread on the top or of the top thread on the bottom. It is important that you rely on both your sense of touch and your sense of sight. Sight alone can be deceived by stitches that appear pretty on the front but hide ugliness on the back. Learn to rely on your fingertips as a backup for determining the right tension.

Top Tension Adjustments

Don't be afraid of this tension dial; it is your friend.

Ugly top stitches appear on the front of your work when the top tension is too tight. The bobbin thread is pulled up so that it is visible among the stitches on the front. It appears as little dots and is especially obvious when the bobbin thread color differs from that of the top thread. So when bobbin dots are showing, I loosen the top tension by turning the dial slightly to the left. Always make slight adjustments to your tension dial; a little bit goes a long way. When making tension adjustments, I always remind myself: "Righty tighty, lefty loosey." You can further loosen the top tension by bypassing the tension discs altogether.

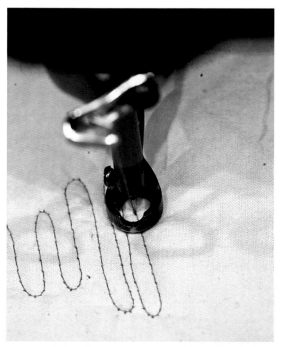

Ugly top stitches: The top tension is too tight, pulling the bobbin thread to the top.

Ugly bottom stitches, which take place under the machine on the backing fabric, can be a bit more challenging to judge as you quilt. However, both top and bottom stitches are equally important to the life and functionality of a quilt. Consider them a team, working together to help you produce a high-quality work of art. Keep a flashlight nearby for frequent tension checks on the backing. Check these stitches often, not just when you change threads. A pretty stitch should not show traces of top thread underneath, just the bobbin thread. If the top thread presents itself, usually in loops or bumps, it means that the bobbin thread's tension is overpowering that of the top thread, pulling the top thread to the back. If this is the case, simply tighten your top tension—"righty tighty"—in slight increments until you produce a pretty stitch.

Ugly bottom stitches: The top tension is too loose; it is allowing the bobbin thread to pull it to the back.

Bobbin Tension Adjustments

Unwarranted fear of bobbin tension adjustments prevents many people from living the thread-diverse life they desire. As I said, the top and bottom are a team. Most of the time, the top tension carries the bulk of the responsibility. However, there are many times when the bobbin tension must step up to the plate, loosen up, and save the day.

Let me offer a scenario to help you understand the need for bobbin tension adjustments. Let's say that I am using a temperamental metallic thread that requires very little tension to avoid breakage. To accommodate the thread, I perform my "lefty loosey" twist on the top tension dial until there is virtually no tension. My bobbin tension is currently set by the factory, which provides a fair amount of tension. The bobbin thread is going to grab hold of the top thread and pull it to the back because the top thread has little tension to balance its bobbin teammate. The result will be ugly, weak stitches. The bobbin thread must compromise by letting loose.

The adjustment is very simple. First throw your inhibitions out the window. Then picture the small bobbin tension screw as a clock face and turn it in ten-minute increments to the left. When your stitches are pretty, top and bottom, and your decorative thread is happy, you have selected the perfect adjustment.

You should feel comfortable adjusting the tension of your bobbin; it is very simple to do—"righty tighty, lefty loosey."

 TIP

If you would like to learn more about the properties of thread, how it is made, or any other nitty-gritty thread information, download *A Thread of Truth* at www.ylicorp.com. It is a detailed brochure containing all of the thread facts you could possibly hope for. In addition, www.superiorthreads.com offers in-depth thread education. The thread industry is continually improving and making changes to its products. For updated information, visit thread manufacturers' websites.

Needles

Several different sizes of needles are available to longarm quilters, ranging from beefy industrial types to finer types more like those you'd find on a domestic machine. I keep a wide range of needle sizes on hand because different sizes have different applications. The stronger, larger needles are a good choice for thicker threads, open designs, fast stitching, and so on, while the finer needles are more appropriate for slow-stitched, intricate work. Larger needles produce larger holes, which is often undesirable in custom work. However, too fine a needle cannot withstand vigorous motions.

When troubleshooting, the needle is a great starting point. Often, increasing the needle size alone solves the problem of thread breakage because the eye of the needle is larger, reducing thread friction. In addition, needles may develop burrs or have factory imperfections that can contribute to thread breakage. "Replace, restore, regroup" is my motto for needle troubleshooting. I believe in the importance of frequent needle changes. I usually insert a fresh needle after about eight hours of quilting. It's impossible to create nice stitches with a crowbar.

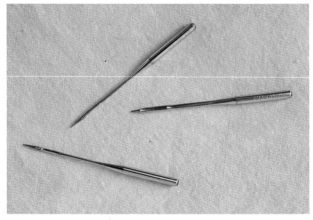

Many different types of needles are available for longarms, ranging from very large to very fine.

Silken Defiance, 65" × 65"

Ready, Set, Quilt!

Backing Fabric Selection

Never underestimate the power of the backing fabric. When I was a fairly new longarm quilter, quilting for hire, I would cringe when my clients would deliver their quilts to me with white sheets selected as their backing fabric. As icing on the cake, they usually preferred that I use dark threads for these particular scenarios. You might wonder why this frightened me so. Well, have you ever heard the phrase "sticks out like a sore thumb"? I was, and probably still am, simply not confident in my ability to quilt an entire piece without a "sore thumb" (mistake). We can use every precaution and check the underside often, yet an occasional loop or tension faux pas may still present itself.

Busy Prints

Busily patterned prints are a great choice for concealing the underside of your work. As a basis for determining the right backing fabric color, consider the thread color(s) that you are likely to use on the top. Because the bobbin and top threads should be similar in color, I like to match my backing and bobbin colors closely. When I plan to incorporate many different thread colors, I will select a backing fabric combining colors similar to those of my planned threads.

Busy prints with high contrast are a great backing fabric choice.

Backing Weave

When selecting backing fabric, also consider thread count. Fabrics that have a softer hand and are more loosely woven are less likely to form aggravating puckers. Puckers are a quilter's bad dream; folds are a quilter's nightmare. They always seem to remain unnoticed until they have been trapped by hundreds of yards of quilting. One interesting quality about little stitches: What takes minutes to put in takes hours to take out. Because of this, I have decided that it is best to take every precaution to avoid puckered disasters.

 TIP

Prewashing your backing fabrics in warm water also will help prevent puckering because it removes the sizing and loosens up the fibers a bit.

Backing Preparation

It is very important that your backing fabric is cut squarely. A squared-up backing will roll up evenly onto the machine, reducing the emergence of puckers and folds. Don't rely on the fabric shop to cut your fabric straight. Fabric is often wound onto the bolt less than perfectly, resulting in imperfect or angled cuts. I always buy generous amounts of my selected backing fabric. Several inches may need to be removed to create a squared piece. In addition, you should always allow at least 5″ excess along both sides, the top, and the bottom. If the backing requires combined pieces to meet the size requirement, seam the pieces and then square it up as one.

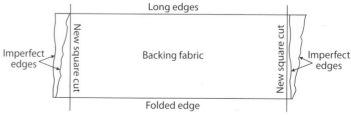

To square up the backing fabric, fold the 2 long edges together and then make clean 90° cuts at both ends.

Batting Selection

Batting gives life to our work!

Batting is the heart of the quilt. It gives life to our creative labors and provides warmth and comfort to those who wrap up in our quilts. I believe in choosing high-quality battings from reputable manufacturers. They should feel nice on their own, outside the quilt. You will want to choose your batting based on the planned quilting design and the intended use of the quilt. If you plan to quilt loosely, with stitching far apart, refer to the package to ensure that the batting will remain intact with fewer supportive stitches. Here are some of the battings that I use and love.

Wool

Hobbs wool batting is at the top of my list. It meets all of my quilting needs, so I use it most of the time. In my opinion, it has the perfect amount of loft. It allows the quilting designs to "pop" even without the addition of trapunto. I use it for both utility and show quilts. Wool is pleasing for utility quilts because it is a natural insulator, providing the right amount of warmth. Hobbs wool batting has a resin bonding that helps prevent bearding, which happens when the fibers of the batting work their way through to the quilt's surface. (This happened once to a show quilt of mine with polyester batting. After that, I switched to wool and haven't experienced unsightly bearding since.)

Another benefit of wool batting is its minimal crease retention. This is an important factor to consider for those, like me, who dabble in show quilting. Show quilts must be willing to travel from show to show, across the country. This means that they must be folded and placed in a small box for days at a time. It is always a relief to see your quilt hanging in the show the way you sent it—flat and crease-free.

Wool batting produces an appropriate amount of loft in quilting designs.

Cotton

There was a time when I only had eyes for cotton. Though I have expanded my views some, I still revisit this tried-and-true fiber often. Cotton seems like the right choice in batting because its content matches that of the majority of our quilting fabric. Like wool, it's wonderful to sleep under and wrap up in because of its breathability as a natural fiber. I particularly like to use it when a low-loft, bulk-free result is desired, as with utility or home décor quilts. It lacks the unmistakable puff of a high-loft polyester batting. For this reason, it is a great choice for art or wall quilts that need to hang flat against the wall. Another great characteristic of cotton batting is its surface texture. Quilt tops adhere to it nicely, which prevents migration or shifting of the quilt top during the quilting process (which can happen with slippery battings).

Do note that cotton batting shrinks. This, however, can add to its appeal because after washing, quilts with cotton batting take on the antiqued look desired by many, especially traditionalists. The shrinkage also can be helpful in concealing the occasional mistake or uneven stitches because the actual stitch line becomes hidden, buried by the shrinkage. If you would like to use cotton batting but don't want it to alter your quilted result, prewash the batting, avoiding agitation, before using it. Machine dry the batting for additional preshrinkage.

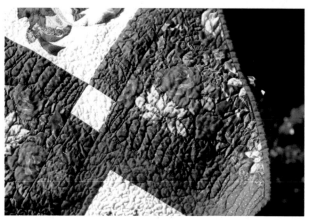

Cotton battings shrink and can add an antique feel to your quilts once they are washed.

Silk

Washable silk batting is a relatively new product. I have used it many times in both show and utilitarian applications. It is similar to polyester batting in its lightweight, airy qualities. Unlike polyester, however, silk is a natural fiber, possessing the breathable, insulating qualities desired in bed quilts. Its supple hand and beautiful drape are unparalleled. I enjoy using it in quilted garments for this reason.

Combinations

You can combine similar or different batting types to produce desired effects, such as additional loft or added weight. I like to combine wool with cotton for the best of both worlds. I usually prewash both battings to prevent future uneven shrinkage. I place the cotton closest to the backing fabric and the wool on top. The wool gives my quilting designs the loft they need while the cotton adds weight. The added weight contributes stability for the successful hanging sought after for wall and show presentations.

Quilt Loading

Quilt loading is the final step before the real fun begins. I pin my quilts directly to the machine's canvas leaders. Zippered leaders are a great option if you plan to remove the quilt from the machine prior to its completion, in the case of sharing the machine or alternating work. I used to share a machine with my mom, and we would use zippered leaders to accommodate one another. Nowadays, I focus my attention on one quilt at a time, so I don't find it necessary to use zippered leaders. The preparation time involved in applying the zippered leaders to the quilt is equal to the pinning time, so I choose to eliminate the extra step. It is easy to get eager as the quilting process draws near, but don't cut corners at this point—proper quilt loading will reduce bumps in the quilting road ahead. Most often, I pin the longest edges to the machine to reduce rolling time.

 TIP

The machine's canvas leaders should come premarked at the centers. I add additional measurements to my leaders from the centers out. This extra step is a precautionary measure that helps to maintain a squared-up quilt.

Numbered markings can help keep a quilt squared up.

Always lay the 3 layers out on the floor (or other large, flat area) in order—backing, batting, quilt top. Make certain that you have allowed an excess of at least 5″ per edge on both the batting and the backing pieces.

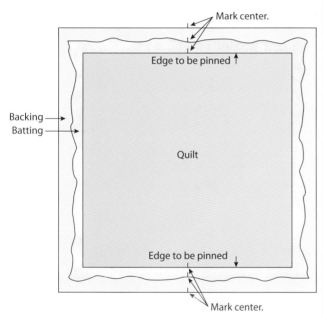

Note the measurements of the edges you plan to pin. Mark the centers of the to-be-pinned edges for all 3 layers.

Pin the three layers of the upper edge to the leader, matching the center marks and outer edge measurements. If you would like additional space at the upper edge for easier stitching or binding applications, simply drop the edge of the quilt down a few inches and then pin or baste.

If you would like extra space, drop the top down from the backing and batting layers, and then pin or baste it in place.

Flip the quilt top and batting to the back so you can focus on loading and rolling the backing fabric accurately. Pin the bottom edge of the backing fabric to the backing leader, matching the centers and outer edge markings. Now that both upper and lower edges are pinned, you are ready to begin rolling. Let the loose backing fabric hang between the bars—it may touch the floor. Roll slowly, keeping the fabric straight and smoothing often to prevent wrinkles from developing. Keep the width of the fabric taut so the edges line up evenly after each advancement of the rolling process.

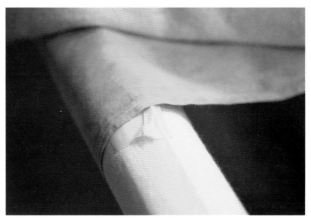

The edges of the backing fabric should line up evenly as you roll.

 TIP

It is important that the floor beneath your machine be cleaned often to prevent objects from clinging to the batting or backing as the fabric brushes the floor. I use a new toilet brush to collect stray threads from my carpet, and then I run the vacuum to prevent unwanted debris from making its way into my quilt. I once stitched a small leaf into a quilt accidentally. The leaf remains to this day, adding a bit of texture to the piece and serving as a reminder to keep things tidy.

Spread the batting over the taut backing fabric evenly. This is a good time to check for clinging threads or other objects that could become trapped in the quilting.

Pin the remaining edge of the quilt top to the leader, matching the centers and outer edge markings. Roll the edge up slowly, as with the backing, keeping it smooth and wrinkle-free. Keep the edges even as you roll the quilt up.

 TIP

When rolled up, the layers should be snug but have some shock absorbency. If you drop your scissors on the quilt and they launch across the room, it's a good indication that the quilt layers are rolled too tightly.

Basted Temporary Border

If the edges of a quilt are critical, as with pieced borders, you can create some breathing room by basting a temporary muslin border along the edges. This enables you to stitch very close to the edge of the border without distorting the shape or hitting obstacles (clamps, pins, runners, and so on). Also, this piece can serve as a practice space or for last-minute tension checks.

 TIP

The pinned lower edge of a quilt can present an occupational hazard at certain positions. Many times, I have caught myself in the belly with the sharp tip of a pin as I was quickly moving from side to side—a rhythm buster to say the least. Not only painful but also messy. Blood and quilts are not a great combination. To protect yourself from stains and injury, simply place a strip of masking tape over the row of pins.

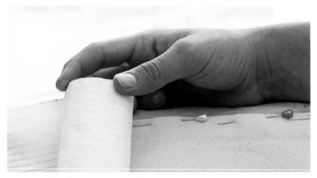

Cover up the dangerous row of pins.

Stops and Starts

"How do you handle your stops and starts?" This might be the most frequently asked question in my classes. It is with confidence that I can share my techniques with you. I can assure you with the utmost honesty, I have never received a bad grade from a quilt show judge in this subject. We all desire a quilt that is visually pleasing, but the quilt's strength and life expectancy are also important. Once we place the intended stitches in our quilt, we expect them to stay. Here are a couple of methods for you to try.

Tiny stitches: This is the method I use most often. It is a good choice for most of the thread weights you will likely be using. Simply take three tiny stitches prior to takeoff using the single-stitch button, and then proceed. When you come to the end of the quilting path, stop. Take three tiny stitches, again with the single-stitch button, and then clip the thread. Trust me; those threads aren't going to escape. Have you ever made a mistake where small stitches were involved and then tried to remove them? It is not easy—those little stitches are stubborn and difficult to dislodge.

Buried threads: If you have selected a heavy thread weight or are stitching open designs in which stops and starts will be obvious, you might choose to bury the thread ends into the layers using a hand needle. This is quite a bit more time consuming than simply taking tiny stitches, but the results are very clean. I use a self-threading hand needle to avoid the eye strain that might develop after numerous rethreads.

If you have further quilting planned for the quilt, you can secure the two thread tails (top and bobbin) by burying them in the middle of your quilt sandwich. Direct the threads toward spaces to be quilted and they will be held securely in place when that area is quilted.

If no further quilting will be done in the vicinity, you may wish to pull the thread tails to the back side and secure them with a knot, a dab of liquid seam sealant, or both. This technique is also useful when the top contains light-colored fabrics that thread tails might show through.

Muscle Fatigue

Though we don't work up a sweat, burn many calories, or develop a six-pack of abdominal muscles, intense longarm quilting can wreak havoc on those muscles of ours. Oh, the aches and pains of longarm quilting—you would think that we had just tilled five acres of land! I must admit I have learned the hard way that there are things our muscles appreciate and things they abhor. Here is my list:

Muscles Appreciate

- Stretching before, during, and after quilting
- Staying hydrated with water
- Taking frequent breaks (If you are drinking lots of water, then frequent breaks will come naturally!)
- Shifting your weight
- Resting

Muscles Abhor

- Tight gripping of the machine handles (white-knuckle syndrome)
- Bad posture (hunching over)
- Talking on the phone while quilting (Holding the phone with a hunched shoulder is a definite no-no; if you must talk on the phone, use a headset.)
- Becoming dehydrated or famished because you can't bear to step away from the machine
- Remaining in the same stance for prolonged periods of time
- Sleeplessness

Giving In to Sleep

Ah, the need for sleep—a driven quilter's worst enemy. I find fatigue to be quite an inconvenience and often wish that I could survive on just one hour of sleep per night so that I could get an extra seven hours of quilting in before morning. Unfortunately, this is not the case for me and probably isn't for you either. Accepting that your body needs rest to restore and repair itself is crucial to the production of quality work. Our job involves a great deal of skill. It demands an alert mind and good reactions. When your blinks and yawns outnumber your stitches, it's time to call it a night. By pushing yourself to work in an overtired state, you open the door for mistakes. When you give your quilt the fresh, rested talent it deserves, you will be rewarded tenfold!

Masquerade, 63" × 63"

Postquilting

Blocking is the magic restorer in the postquilting process and requires many pins to help manipulate the quilt into perfect shape.

Nothing compares with the sense of accomplishment that comes over us as we take that final stitch. Sometimes a quilt's completion is bittersweet as we think of the fun and joy that went into its creation. I always look forward to removing the quilt from my machine, but I still like to take a few last precautions to ensure that the quilting really is finished. Too many times, I have eagerly pulled the pins out, flopped the quilt onto the floor, and then noticed a bare, missed section staring up at me. Frustration is an understatement. Now, instead of getting ahead of myself, I take these extra steps that assist in spotting unquilted, overlooked spaces:

- I loosen the leaders, allowing the quilt to hang loosely to the front.

- I examine the quilt both up close and from a distance for inconsistencies.

- I change the direction of the light. I use a flashlight to light the quilt from the side. Side lighting exaggerates texture, so areas lacking quilting will become obvious.

Fabrics and batting have astonishing manipulative qualities. Your quilt will be better than new when you are finished blocking it.

Quilt Blocking

We care, we toil, we safeguard, but when all is said and done, we distort. As perfect as our seams once were, sometimes "shift happens." Borders may take on a wavy appearance along the seamlines; blocks may rebel—too hip to be square.

All is not lost, though; there is one last step—blocking. I like to think of blocking as the magic restorer. I am always amazed at the power held by water and a little bit of manipulation. Right from the quilt's conception, I plan for this process.

Migrating dyes

I know that the quilt is going to be heavily saturated, so I take the measures needed to make certain bleeding won't occur. Water is the only ingredient needed to cause loose dyes to migrate to a neighboring fabric. Hand-dyed fabrics are especially prone to dye release. If you suspect bleeding might be an issue, you can opt out of blocking altogether or try washing the quilt with warm water and Synthrapol (page 127). Using this product to wash your quilt either by hand (in the bathtub) or in a washing machine will allow the dyes to release into the water, where they will become diluted and less likely to color or tint nearby fabrics.

Let's Block

Supplies Needed

- Measuring tape (I use the industrial type that locks.)
- Sprayer (Get a new sprayer like the kind sometimes used for garden chemicals. Be sure to label it *quilt* so you don't mistakenly spray chemicals onto your quilt.)
- Pins
- Large square ruler
- Blocking surface

Preparing

1. Lay the quilt on the blocking surface.

2. Thoroughly soak the quilt with clean water using a clean sprayer. The quilt should be very wet. Large quilts may require more than a gallon of water for adequate soaking.

3. Pat the quilt to distribute the water into its layers. You are ready to reshape.

Reshaping

1. Begin with the quilt's width. Using the tape measure, take measurements of the edges, the middle, and the points halfway between. Write down these 5 measurements and figure their average.

2. Pin the 2 side edges of the quilt to the blocking surface so that they meet this measurement. If a section falls short of the measurement slightly, gently pull the edge until it meets it. If it exceeds the measurement, push the edge inward.

3. Repeat for the quilt's length.

4. Now that your quilt's outer edges are squared up, you are ready to reshape any portions that have become mis-shapen. I usually begin at the corners. Lay the square ruler over a corner. Realign the border seam with the straight guides of the square ruler by gently manipulating the fabric.

5. Once the seam has become straightened, thoroughly pin it in place.

6. Repeat for the remaining corners, the sashing, and the blocks.

Use plenty of pins. They will secure your fixes and encourage the quilt to dry in the proper shape. If you notice hilly areas, rewet and then pat to flatten. You can expedite the drying process by running a fan or opening windows, weather permitting. Now, step aside and let the transformation take place. It usually takes at least 24 hours for a blocked quilt to dry, so be patient. You can visit your quilt, peek at it, pat it, tell it your hopes and dreams, but do not remove the pins until the drying is complete.

BLOCKING SURFACE

I have fashioned a design wall for my studio that also serves as my blocking surface. When it is performing its design wall duties in an upright position, it is held in place loosely by corsage pins. When it is ready to play the role of the blocking surface, I remove the pins and lay it flat on the floor. Though plastic-covered carpeting would suffice, I would hesitate to block a quilt there because the moisture could cause even undetected floor odors to be absorbed into the quilt.

Here are the simple instructions for creating a fabulous, double-duty blocking surface.

MATERIALS NEEDED:

- Foamcore board (I have 2 separate pieces that I place together, each measuring 8′ × 3′.)
- Cotton batting or flannel (at least 6″ larger per side than the foamcore board)
- Duct tape

Cover one side of the foamcore board (each piece separately, if you have 2 pieces like I do) with the cotton batting or flannel. Wrap it snugly and secure the edges of the batting to the back side of the board using duct tape. You are in business.

Binding

Proper binding technique is essential to a nice, flat-edged quilt. It is especially important in quilts that will hang on a wall or in a quilt show, though it is also conducive to a lovely drape in a bed quilt. The extra time spent to create a good binding will prove to be a worthwhile investment. Don't sprint to the finish line. Follow these steps for a great binding:

1. Establish the seam allowance needed for your desired binding width and the size you should cut your fabric to achieve it. Depending on the thickness of the quilt at the edge, it may be necessary to adjust the seam allowance a skosh. Here are a couple of starting points:

- Narrow binding—2″ strip with ¼″ seam allowance

- Wide binding—3″ strip with ½″ seam allowance

2. Create a sample using the exact materials used in your original—fabrics and batting. The binding should be evenly filled by the contents of the seam allowance. After the binding is stitched to the front and turned to the back, the folded edge should meet up with the stitch line perfectly. Adjust the needle position to obtain the right seam allowance.

3. Create a continuous length of binding by sewing together enough fabric strips to exceed the perimeter of the quilt by approximately 2′. The excess fabric will be needed for the mitered corners and will provide you with some breathing room for joining the edges. Fold the strip in half lengthwise with wrong sides together. Press.

4. Measure both the length and the width of the quilt in the same 5 places you measured for blocking: edges, middle, and halfway between. Make note of the smallest of the 5 measurements for both width and length.

First edge

5. Mark the binding strip at the measurement noted from your quilt measurement. Also mark the center of the binding at the quilt's edge.

6. Pin the right side of the binding to the quilt top along this first edge, matching the marks on the binding with the quilt's center marks and the corners. It may be necessary to ease in fullness along the quilt's edge so the binding will fit. If easing is needed, avoid doing so near the corners. Allow 5″ or more from the corner in each direction before you begin easing. Easing close to the corners may cause them to flip out and not hang flat.

7. Begin sewing this first edge about a quarter of the way down from the corner. When you come to the next corner, miter it.

Finishing

8. Measure the binding strip from the mitered corner to the length noted in your quilt's measurement, and then mark.

9. Pin the binding to the quilt, matching the centers and lining up the quilt's edge with the binding mark.

10. Sew. Miter the next corner.

11. Repeat until the binding is sewn to all of the quilt's edges.

12. Join the ends of the binding strip at a 45° angle.

13. Hand sew the binding strip to the back side of the quilt, matching the folded edge of the binding to the stitch line.

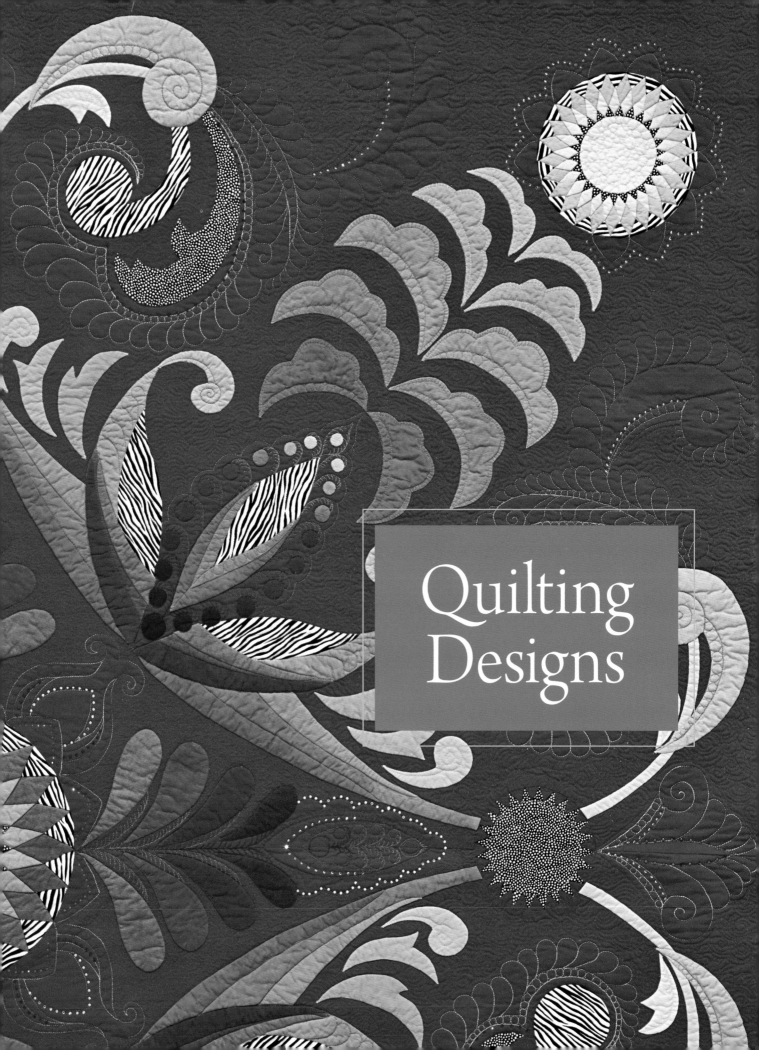

Quilting
Designs

Totem Tango

Daydream

Daydream corner

Polynesian Pastime

Polynesian Pastime corner

Harmony

August Arrival

Crazy for Cupcakes

Crazy for Cupcakes corner

Serendipity

My Eyes Adore You

My Eyes Adore You corner

Arabesque

Arabesque corner

Bora Bora

Simplicity

September Journey

Tree of Love

May Flowers

Flightful Ambition

Royal Crown

Flamingo Flair

La Bella Vita

Le Cirque

June Bloom

Tiara

Tiara corner

Fairy Tale

Open Sky

Jitterbug

Que Sera Sera

A Touch of Tuscany

A Visit to Tuscany

Crazy Eights

Creeping Vine

Garden of Eden

Garden of Eden corner

A Splash of Silken Defiance

Tuscan Flourish

Reminisce corner

About the Author

Gina Perkes is an internationally known, award-winning quilter and creator of wearable art. She was honored with the International Quilt Association's Future of Quilting Award. Gina has been quilting for more than a decade and has managed to successfully balance her quilting passion with her role as the mother of three children. She is featured in Gammill Quilting Systems' quilting ads and is proud to represent the company as a national spokesperson. She has appeared on several quilting television shows, including *Linda's Longarm Quilters* and *The Quilt Show*. Gina travels throughout the country teaching and giving trunk shows. She loves working with other quilters, sharing her techniques and helping them find inspiration and gain confidence.

Resources

Teaching information and supplies

Gina Perkes
gperkes.fatcow.com

Longarm machines and accessories

Gammill Quilting Systems
www.gammill.com
800-659-8224

Threads

Fil-Tec, Inc.
www.fil-tec.com
www.bobbincentral.com
800-258-5052
Magna-Glide prewound bobbins

Sew-Art International
www.sewartinternational.com
800-231-2787
Monofilament

Superior Threads
www.superiorthreads.com
800-499-1777
Polyester monofilament, Trilobal, The Bottom Line, thread education

YLI Corporation
www.ylicorp.com
803-985-3100
Thread education

Pencils and pens

Westek, Inc.
www.sewline-product.com

Rulers and notions

The Gadget Girls
www.thegadgetgirls.com
888-844-8537

C-Thru Ruler Company
www.cthruruler.com
Flexible rulers for drafting and marking

Sulky of America
www.sulky.com
800-874-4115
Solvy

Laundering and dye treatment products

PRO Chemical & Dye
www.prochemicalanddye.com
Synthrapol

Great Titles and Products

from C&T PUBLISHING and stashBOOKS®

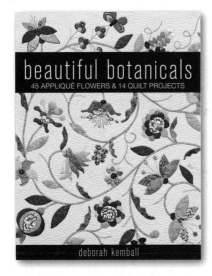

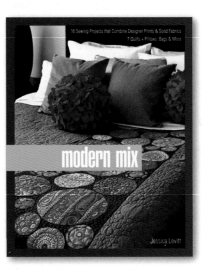

Available at your local retailer or **www.ctpub.com** *or* **800-284-1114**